Maude Egerton Hine King

Round about a Brighton coach office

Maude Egerton Hine King

Round about a Brighton coach office

ISBN/EAN: 9783337175214

Printed in Europe, USA, Canada, Australia, Japan

Cover: Foto ©Andreas Hilbeck / pixelio.de

More available books at **www.hansebooks.com**

JOHN·LANE'S·ARCADY·LIBRARY

·ROUND·ABOUT·A· ·BRIGHTON·COACH·OFFICE·

Round About A Brighton Coach Office

BY
Maude Egerton King

Illustrated By
Lucy Kemp-Welch

LONDON
John Lane The Bodley Head
New York
Macmillan & Co
1896

Printed by BALLANTYNE, HANSON & Co.
At the Ballantyne Press

To the
Memory of my Father
HENRY GEORGE HINE
In whose character, under another name, I here try
to tell others all that he so often told me about
the people and places of his youth, and
to whose tender heart, retentive mind,
and happy gift of telling I
owe whatever is of
worth in
them,
I dedicate this handful of
true stories

CONTENTS

Chapter I
The Brighton of My Boyhood   *Page*   1

Chapter II
The Coachmaster   31

Chapter III
Miss Patten's School   91

Chapter IV
Our Gentleman Boarder   107

Chapter V
A Day of Punishment   139

Contents

Chapter VI
My Pretty Sister   *Page* 161

Chapter VII
Our Odd-Men   173

Chapter VIII
Sukie   197

Driving the Young Ladies on their Rounds to the Toy-shops	Frontispiece
Rank and Fashion at Brighton	Page 1
Guests at the Pavilion	7
The Dress and Bearing of the Great Ladies	22
He often looked over the Hedge and saw the Coach go by	31
At the Head of the Plough	32
An Awkward Handful	39
Patting them and Feeling their Legs	43
Her Little Nosegay	47
The Dashing Style	49
A Sussex Lane	53

List of Illustrations

What's it all about ?	Page 57
An Unreliable Witness	71
The two Oldest and most Beloved	73
The Meeting of Creditors	77
Walking amongst the Flowers	83
Miss Patten's School	91
Set off for a Ten Miles' Drive	93
Clung to Him with Rapture touched with Despair	101
Our Gentleman Boarder	107
It looked as Dainty as you please	115
He won my Mother's Heart	119
A Day of Punishment	139
The Stool of Repentance	147
A Little Dancing Party	161
In Her little Glass and China Shop	163
The Roads were in a Terrible Condition	173
Touched the Hat several Times	181
Sukie	197
My Father had nowhere to Fold his Cravat	207
Alert and Union	209

Chapter 1

THE BRIGHTON OF MY BOYHOOD

THERE may be those who, seeing the title of this little book, will at once suppose they have alighted on a story of Brighton as it is to-day—the gay, big Brighton of the speculative hotel-proprietor and music-hall manager. Therefore I will in fairness tell them, and without more ado, that of this Brighton I have never a word to say. I am an old man now, and like many another of my kind I have an excellent memory and a clinging affection for the things that happened in times long gone, and so I am only going to gossip about the Brighton I knew and loved as a little boy ; of which,

The Brighton of my Boyhood

and the simple kindly life that was lived in it, there is little now left, and what there is is being daily elbowed out of existence by a veritable plague of improvements.

Possibly you will be wondering how long ago I was a little boy?

One day when I was just the same height as the key-hole of the office-door, I sat out in our cobble-stoned yard where the clothes were drying, with my cat beside me. I was holding him down gently but firmly upon three nest-eggs borrowed from my mother's hen-coops. Very earnestly I awaited the hatching-out, whether of kits or chicks I was puzzled to know, any little live fluffy creatures would have been equally welcome and dear to me. Then the wash-house door opened, and Sukie came out with her arms full of clothes.

"Harry," she said, putting down her basket, "Have 'ee heard the news?" And she flicked at my puss as he escaped my hold and trotted softly into the house. "The old King's dead at last, Harry," she went on, with a clothes-peg in her mouth, her hands busily fixing the linen on the line over her head. Whereupon, to her great surprise, I cried bitterly, for though I had heard little, and thought less, about the King, it seemed to me very sad that he

The Brighton of my Boyhood

should die. A little while after they gave me a medal of his late Majesty King George III. in the kind of wig he ordinarily wore, going up to Heaven, assisted by an angel and greeted by the words, "Well done, thou good and faithful servant," issuing from a cloud. And so for the when-a-bouts of my childhood I will ask you to go and look in your history-book.

My Brighton was a little town of a few thousand inhabitants, which had been growing up around the old fishing-village of Brighthelmstone ever since a great London doctor had begun to send his royal and noble patients to regain in sea-air and sea-bathing the strength they wasted in the racket of London life. The principal streets were Church Street and North Street running through the town from east to west, the latter taking a large curve northwards towards Henfield after passing the church. Out of North Street Great Russell Street, West Street, Middle Street, Ship Street, East Street ran southwards to the sea—some of them so downhill that as you went down the brick foot-ways the exuberant scent of the sea came up to greet you, and you saw it shimmer and heave at the end of the street. At the

The Brighton of my Boyhood

east end of North Street lay Castle Square, the ever-stirring scene of the goings and comings of the several coaches. Passing beyond this you came out upon the Steine, a beautiful greensward granted to Dutch refugee fishermen in Queen Elizabeth's time, for the drying of nets and harbouring of boats. On the south it lay open to the sea, looking north you had a peep of Hollingbury Hill; on its western side stood the pretty mansions of Mrs. Fitzherbert and other distinguished persons, while the eastern was as yet little built upon. This grassy space contributed greatly to the pleasant appearance of the sea-front. Such houses too as were then built along the cliff were good of their kind; they were of modest though varying heights, and were often constructed of water-worn flints cemented in mortar, and they had bowed glass windows of many panes. Of the inns here, or otherwhere in the town, the "Old Ship" ranked as far and away the most stylish. Along the cliff, and in front of these buildings, ran a roadway (in places only a footway) edged with a wooden paling and connected here and there with the beach by a rough-and-ready set of wooden stairs. Russell Street was the most westerly limit of my Brighton,

The Brighton of my Boyhood

and so, too, when you passed east of the Steine, Brighton ceased to be, and you were in open country from there to Rottingdean.

And in the foreground of this old Brighton lay the beach full of the quaint life and business of the fishery folk. There, dotted about, stood the rope-shops, little huts made from the fore-parts of disused hog-boats, in which the fishermen stored their nets and ropes and many a wholesome tarry-smelling thing proper to their trade. Nets in tangled heaps, or widely spread for the drying, lay all about, craving careful stepping of the unaccustomed visitor. Here the fishermen, brawny fellows with hair falling to their very shoulders from under their red caps, and great boots more than knee high and meeting their full petticoats, tarred their boats, mended their nets or lolled against the great capstans, pipe in mouth. There, at the doors of the rope-shops the older among them, some so old that they had done with going to sea, sat in the sun and patched the russet and ruddy sails. And the brown beach-children threw ducks and drakes at the water's edge and played among the idle boats in which some day they too must put out to the perilous harvesting.

The Brighton of my Boyhood

On the spot where to-day the Aquarium stands, the fishermen held their market; and there, among a picturesque confusion of wicker creels, heaped nets, and the silver hillocks of writhing fish, you might hear some very fine bargaining between the townsmen and the fisher-folk. And if, to your thinking, bulk and lung-power indicated superiority, you would unquestionably have backed the latter; and yet it not unseldom happened that a quiet determination to secure the best at the lowest price, would outlast a deal of honest bluster and the broadest Sussex bawl.

Down among the simple beach-folk there came from time to time the beaux and butterflies who were guests at the Pavilion, and sometimes the King himself. The burly fishermen accepted the petting and patronising with amused toleration; they taught the gentlemen to swim and grinned at their first flounderings: and they spoke of their anointed sovereign as "Jarge." The daintiest ladies delivered themselves delightedly into the hands of the fat bathing women in their short petticoats, and, were they duchesses or daughters of half-pay captains, submitted merrily to their duckings and dousings, and

The Brighton of my Boyhood

accepted as part of this charming topsy-turvy life by the sea that the old creatures should scold them for their venturesomeness and hail them each as "my dear."

That *was* a place to be a child in, that old Brighton of mine! If it were granted me to live again the first years of my life in any place of my choice, I would first beg the loan of a magical wand, and waving it

The Brighton of my Boyhood

over Brighton, rid it of its nightmare of Ally Sloperism; and when the homely, happy little town had reasserted itself, I would go back up and down the brick-paved streets, and down among the boats on the beach, and live my merry healthy life over again.

And yet what were the old place without the old company? "Ah, all are gone, the old familiar faces," parents, sisters, brothers, cousin Ridley, Sukie, and even Tim Hurst, for all the charmed life he brought through so many a sea-peril. And when I think of that, I do not want the old time back, save here upon paper, where I can at will bring the dear ones all about me again.

Yes, it certainly was the place to be a boy in. We had all the beach and some of the sea for our playground, and from babyhood we were ruddied with sun and salt air, seasoned with countless sea-drenchings, and so rendered as wholesome and weatherproof as boys could be. It is true we saw an example of very rough-and-ready manners, and heard many strong words among our friends the fishermen and the manlike fisher-lads; but we took little harm of them. And, on the other hand, I know it was an undoubted good for us as growing lads to have such sort

The Brighton of my Boyhood

for our friends and comrades: men who lived in such untroubled if unexpressed faith within constant sound of the sea, from which, in frequent peril of death, they must wrest their means of livelihood; who at the call of distress would get up from sleep, or lay aside their pipes, as it were all a part of the day's work, and though the sea should fling their boats a dozen times back on the beach, win out at length by sheer strength of heart through the fury of wind and wave—to return, if God willed, with a burden of precious human wreckage, perchance to return no more at all.

Old Master Hurst and his three sons (giants in size and strength were all the four of them) had saved more lives, it was said, than any other ten on Brighton beach; but if you questioned them on the matter they were shy as children, and did you press them to relate but one of their stirring adventures, would invariably ask you, had you ever heard of their grandmother, old Mis' Hurst, who was reported the strongest woman 'long all the coast in her time; for by simply sitting down and pulling at a rope, with her heels dug deep into the sand, she could haul up a boat as well as any capstan.

The Brighton of my Boyhood

"How many did ye say there was of them, father?" roared Tim Hurst when, at our earnest request, he took us into his rope-shop to show us his greatest treasure. This was a testimonial presented to his father and brothers by a number of persons they had rescued from a wreck one bitter night—a large roll of parchment, whereon were the signatures of those saved, surmounted by a deal of handsome and totally illegible blazoning in red, blue, and gold, which we all took on faith as expressive of their gratitude, admiring it hugely.

"Thirt'-nine and a dog," said old Master Hurst, who was smoking with closed eyes in the sun outside.

"Well, *I* say forty and a dog," roared Tim again.

"Thirt'-nine's the figger, I tell ye, boy," growled the old giant, opening one eye and peering in at us; "and don't go pilin' up reckonin's in that way, or mebbe th' Almighty won't let ye do the like again."

The fisher-folk were quite able to stand up for their rights in those days, and fought sturdily against every encroachment of the growing health resort on the old fishing-town; and on the strength of their ancient right to draw boats up on to the Steine in rough weather, granted them, they claimed,

The Brighton of my Boyhood

by Queen Elizabeth, they made but short work of the railings which the Town Council, with an eye to the more private promenading of fashionable visitors, planted round its pleasant greensward. They had their way for the time, but they could not prove their claim; and so in the end the railings, and one by one the other improvements, came in, and thrust aside the old fishery, for all its stubborn traditions and unproveable rights, and built up the Brighton we have to-day.

The fishermen were a great feature in the keeping of Christmas in old Brighton, for on Christmas Eve they went about the town with lanterns, singing carols and old-fashioned hymns. It was always our custom, when they reached our part of East Street, to listen to at least one carol before we admitted them, just for the pleasure of hearing the voices on the fine air; and then to welcome them into the coach-office. At the opening of the door they called out their seasonable greetings, and began stamping the snow off their great boots, the light of their lanterns showing their breath on the frosty air and catching them beneath noses and chins in a way that rendered the best-known face strange and grotesque. And then they came clumping in with:

The Brighton of my Boyhood

"How be you, Mast'r 'Yde, sir?"

"Hopes you're pretty well, Mrs. 'Yde, ma'am?"

"Nicely, thank you, Speedwell Jasper, and how are you?"

And when all were gathered in, one would always say, "We've just looked in to sing you a little song, Mast'r 'Yde, if you please, sir."

And so after such preliminary coughing, humming, and hoarse whispering as they deemed proper to the occasion, they let out their great voices, not altogether unmovingly, in those time-honoured Christmas songs, "Christians, awake, arise, rejoice, and sing;" "God rest you, merry gentlemen," and many another. There was also one purely secular song, which they evidently fancied hugely. It was a kind of rough love song; but I remember nothing of it now save the first line, which they gave with great gusto, "No di'monds was so br-i-ight." One of their company beat out the time with his great forefinger and slow wagging of the head. They sang very loudly, very slowly, retaining a hold on the last note of each verse as long as ever breath allowed. But we would not have had the singing altered even for the better, so good it was in its heartiness and

The Brighton of my Boyhood

simplicity and the glow of an old-world Christmastide. The carolling over, my Mother brought out spiced ale and Christmas cake, and my Father gave each man a coin ; and so with many wishes for a merry Christmas on both sides, out they tramped again into the still frosty night.

There was hardly a man among these fishermen (and yet for the most part they were as honest a set of fellows as heart could wish) that was not something of a smuggler ; and there was not a soul among us Brighton folk, from the King himself to the straitest Quaker of the Black Lion Street Meeting, but was glad enough to buy the smuggled goods. I do not know they were always of the superior quality boasted by their vendors, but that their contraband character added a zest to their original worth, there can be no doubt at all ; it lent a fine aroma to our cognac, it spiced the tobacco in our pipes and tinged a silken gown with the glamour of romance.

The ugly stories of encounters between coastguards and smugglers, some of them stories of an inhumanity rare, as I like to believe, in our dear England, had died into history in my childhood. Smuggling had become so barefaced and was so per-

The Brighton of my Boyhood

sistently supported by the townsfolk in Brighton and otherwhere, that there was nothing for it but for the excisemen to wink at it as often as possible, very occasionally make a show of resistance, and at the worst clap a culprit into gaol for a few weeks by way of reminder that the law of Protection did yet exist, if only to be broken! There was not, I believe, a housewife in all the town but knew where to get her tea and brandy without paying duty, nor a lady that had not learned the trick of considerably reducing the outlay of her pin-money over " real French " fineries, without curtailing her stock of silks and laces at all; nor an innkeeper that would not wink as he assured you, you could not get such cognac as his at *that* price elsewhere! Indeed every gipsy and pedlar-wife would boast in strictest confidence, that she had the very pick of forbidden continental fruit stowed away beneath her homely wares. One such I remember well. She was an old woman who came round selling fowls, butter and eggs in a basket covered with a white cloth. She had glittering eyes, and brass rings in her ears, and a tongue off which the lies and the blarney rolled as easily as rain off a tulip leaf. When my Mother spied her

The Brighton of my Boyhood

coming she invariably cried, with a little pretence of vexation, " Dear, dear, there's that poor old creature come again! Are the spoons out of sight, Susan?" adding sometimes a little apologetically, " Not but what, for all I know, she may be as honest a body as you or I ; and I'm sure a decenter whiter apron I couldn't wish to see." And then, housewife like, she brisked up at the prospect of a little bargain-driving.

"Good morning, m'lady," the wily old gipsy would say, as she entered the kitchen. " Buy a nice fowl, m'dear? Here's a breast for you, did you ever see such a fine fat breast? Just you feel it now!" And then in a hoarse whisper, as Mother or Sukie bent over the basket, " What would you say to a little flask of the very best real French brandy ? or a bit of baccy for the good man, m'lady ; eh, my dear?" and she would raise the wing of an innocent fowl to show the coveted contraband dainties beneath.

But if we little folk fostered the smugglers' trade the great folk came no whit behind. It was an open secret that every extra fine consignment from the Continent found its way first to the Pavilion, that the King might skim the cream off it; while in more than one

The Brighton of my Boyhood

instance the poor fellow that brought it over was fuming his heart out in Lewes gaol.

When a boat laden with such a cargo was expected, the word was passed from one to another of the smuggling brotherhood—often to innkeepers and others in inland villages—that on such a night they would be wanted at such a point along the shore. When she came in they were ready for her, an eager group unlading with all possible speed: some of them, armed with long clubs or "bats," stood on guard around them in a formidable ring. Did the coastguard and his little company appear, these would begin swinging their bats, rendering all approach impossible. For it must be remembered that the law forbade the coastguardsmen to fire until they had lost a man.

One of them, a fine kindly fellow, told me how helpless and foolish he felt with the work going on under his very nose. "I might not fire," he said, "and quite right too; and I could not send a man in among them, as a blow from one of those bats meant certain death." He had had to endure a deal of rough pleasantry from these audacious fellows, he said.

"I advise you to get along home to

The Brighton of my Boyhood

your little beds, gentlemen," sung out an old fisherman on one occasion, amid the appreciative roars of his comrades. "I'm afraid you'll be catching your death o' cold standin' there doing nothing."

"And we took his advice," said my friend.

When the coastguards went, the band would break up in a trice and disperse with the goods according to a before-made plan. Some rode away over the Downs, some made for the nearest village, and others disappeared with a suddenness which suggested the existence of caves there abouts for the storage of treasure.

But my Mother had grim and thrilling tales to tell of the smuggling in her day. A rumour would run from neighbour to neighbour in the little village where she lived, that on such a night a cargo was expected, and that the smugglers were to pass through the village at such o'clock. Then every one went to bed a little earlier than usual, closed their windows and doors, drew their curtains and knew nothing about it. It was the supreme terror of her childhood.

"There was no sleep for me those nights," said my Mother. "I used to say the Lord's Prayer over and over, and then

The Brighton of my Boyhood

just lie and quake in my bed hour after hour. And then I could hear a kind of trampling, only very far off, that came up the leg of my bed into my ear; for in those days the smugglers rode on horseback and all armed, as many as forty together. And then the sound came nearer and nearer till I could hardly breathe, and when at last they came clattering up the street right under my very window, I fairly went under the bed-clothes. Sometimes they stayed a few minutes to drop a few kegs at the 'White Horse,' but they were more like to rush through and out o' the village away and away till I couldn't hear them any more. Though, to be sure, I often thought I could hear them long after I couldn't at all." The morning after, one neighbour would find a little parcel of tea on his threshold, and another a chunk of tobacco, or flask of brandy, which was silently accepted as the fee for good faith and closed lips.

More than once my Mother had heard another trampling, another rush and clatter through the sleeping village, hard on the heels of the first; and then she had cried with terror, for she knew it was a body of excisemen, and that to-morrow all the folk would be talking of a horrid fight some-

The Brighton of my Boyhood

where on the hills ; and one shuddered to think what that might mean, ever since the smugglers had whipped one wretched exciseman to death in Lady Holt Park, and thrown his comrade down the well with his eyes gouged out.

In those days, before the Pavilion had become a third-rate museum and was still a second-rate palace, Brighton did not lack liveliness. The Master of the Ceremonies kept up a round of balls, concerts, card-assemblies, and other polite entertainments throughout the season. To these the Brighton townsfolk and visitors were admitted on payment of a certain sum, and on condition of wearing such-and-such a dress, specified by the M.C. himself. Many of these functions took place in the ballroom of the Castle Tavern, a very gorgeous place in the eyes of Brightonians, decorated, according to the curious wording of the guide-book of that date, " with paintings representing Cupid and Psyche and divers other figures in the ancient grotesque style." They afforded a welcome opportunity for every Tom, Dick, and Harry who could borrow the price of the ticket, to rub shoulders with titled folk, and sometimes with Royalty itself — an opportunity seized upon with no less

The Brighton of my Boyhood

avidity by Mistress Tom, Dick, and Harry, who saw here a fit occasion for airing her last gown of smuggled Lyons silk, and its dainty furbelows of contraband lace from Brussels.

The King had always set the fashion of hob-nobbing with the townspeople, fisher-folk, coach-drivers, shopkeepers, and others, and his friends and guests naturally following his lead, went about the town in among the people, patronising them, flirting with their daughters, and even playing practical jokes upon them with the greatest affability in the world. My Father used to say that when his Majesty was still the Prince Regent, the bearing of himself and his friends in Brighton, while significant of much kindliness of heart and sensible disregard of ceremony, was often not such as to deepen the subjects' reverence for the Throne. There was, unhappily, a certain looseness about the bloods and beaux of Royal set—my Lord Barrymore, Major Hanger, and others—which was by no means an influence for good among the young fellows of our town, who were bound to be in with the fashion, though they should sell their souls for it!

"His Royal Highness would go a long way in those days," my Father used to say,

The Brighton of my Boyhood

"to see a fight between any two countrymen or fishermen that could be bribed to the work. Once I mind 'twas between an ostler and a butcher, and butchery it was if you like. His Royal Highness used to bet very heavy in those days, I heard tell." My father, like all old Brightonians, had many a tale to tell of the Prince's pastimes in our town. Anything in the form of a race had great charms for him, and he was delighted when, for his pleasure, a Captain of the Sussex Militia, mounted by a grenadier of eighteen stone, matched himself to run fifty yards against a pony carrying a feather, to run a hundred and fifty. And the Steine donkey-races were frequently favoured by the Royal presence. The riders, who sometimes rode with their faces to the tails of their steeds, were often gentlemen of noble birth, and once, as gossip says, even princes of the blood.

On the occasion of these Royal romps the Steine was gay with the presence of all the elegant folk from the Pavilion. "The Nobility and Gentry who assemble on this celebrated Promenade," said the bombastic little guide-book of that date, "are not to be equalled for Numbers and Respectability by any in the Kingdom." Thither, too, came the burly fishermen and lads, shouldering

The Brighton of my Boyhood

their way through the dainty crowd to a good stand for seeing, and once there, they nodded, pipe in mouth, good-naturedly

enough to their acquaintances among the aristocracy. There, too, you might see the wives and daughters of the townspeople, prinked out in their very best, and all a-tiptoe

The Brighton of my Boyhood

to study the fashion in the dress and bearing of the great ladies, and ever ready to giggle at and applaud the edifying behaviour of their future Sovereign and his boon companions.

The local journals of the time dwelled lovingly upon the Prince's "elegance of deportment"; and a great London contemporary declared, " The return of the Prince to Brighton has given new life to its collective Population ; Hilarity predominates in the Circles of Fashion, and the rays of Cheerfulness extend to the most humble Purlieus of the Town."

Such doings were by no means over in my time, and for many a day after the public follies of the Regent had disappeared behind the enforced dignity of kingship, we could yet boast of several aristocratic visitors to Brighton who regarded their stay among us, not only as an opportunity for handsome, nay, lavish expenditure, but also as a legitimate occasion for their good-natured, if not very witty, horse-play. Several such cases are still fresh in my mind. For instance, there was one innocent citizen of our town who went to bed one Saturday night as usual, behind a modest white house-front, and awoke in the morning to find it variegated with

The Brighton of my Boyhood

broad stripes of fresh paint in scarlet and blue. Another victim was an old bachelor, a retired leather-merchant from London. He had long rendered himself ridiculous and unpopular by his frequent letters in the local papers, in which he "begged to call attention to" everything, in short, which he did not like, from the ringing of church bells to the playing of children in the streets. He met his reward: and was astounded well-nigh out of his wits on being informed by the early milkwoman, that all his front parlour windows, and his hall door too, were wholly plastered over with advertisements worded thus:

MOTHERS!
Inquire within for Prigg's Patent Panacea Powders for the alleviation of all the Disorders and Diseases incidental to Infancy!

I remember, too, when all Brighton turned out to see the race between the Marquis of Waterford and his friends in invalid carriages drawn by very doddering old men.

The safety and good conduct of our rather rowdy little Brighton was left at nights in the care of the watchmen, Old Charlies, as we called them, who during their perambulations round the town, crying

The Brighton of my Boyhood

the time o' night and the kind of weather, were frequently claimed as lawful prey by the practical jokers who roamed the streets in the small hours. But it must be confessed that, as a rule, these scatter-brained gentlemen paid up very handsomely though anonymously for the privilege of playing their silly pranks. One old fellow I could name had five guinea-pieces left at his lodging the morning after he and his box were so mysteriously carried away into the churchyard and left high and dry on a steep granite tomb.

For the better keeping of peace and order, we boasted a beadle, who was also town crier. Old Catlin was the terror of my childhood, and, as I believe, of many another. The story went, among us youngsters, that he was a monster of malice, consumed with a desire to commit small boys to prison, and fully empowered to do so could he but catch them. The mere glimpse of his ample and gorgeously clad person at the far end of the street so wrought upon my tender mind that there passed before me in horrid procession all my recent misdemeanours and mischiefs, for all the world like a little Judgment Day: and once indeed, when I had just succeeded to a nicety in setting a string-

The Brighton of my Boyhood

trap before a schoolmate's door, the sudden sound of the crier's bell in the next street thrilled me as it had been the last trump itself. Were we balancing along the rails by the cliff edge, the cry " Old Catlin's coming!" swept us down and away in a trice; or playing on the Steine, which in truth we had a perfect right to do, a glimpse of him in the distance sent us flying to the beach; and had the warning note of " Here's old Catlin!" followed us thither, I can answer for one at least that would have run straight into the sea, whither old Catlin, in his yellow stockings and gold braid, dared not follow.

And yet he never caught us, and very like never wished to, nor did I ever meet with any of his victims; and in after years I learned that he was a kindly old fellow, and one that set great store by religion. But history says that he clapped a man into the pillory at the bottom of North Street the very year in which I was born, and perhaps that fact coloured my childish view of him.

And now, lest in my reminiscent rambling I exhaust my readers' charity before ever I come to the people in whose dear memory this little book is to be written, I will, without longer delay, give

The Brighton of my Boyhood

some clue to their several identities. They were very simple people with uneventful histories, and yet such, I think, as may not wholly fail in winning the interest and affection of a kindly hearted reader.

I think we were what people call "a very united family." The thought of a possible death among us crept very early into my mind, and was a secret dread which returned at intervals, generally on Sunday evenings, wet nights, and other dreary seasons for several years: indeed for a long period I privately added to my nightly prayers a petition that we, the whole family including old Sukie and Sprightly the outside porter, might all die in the same moment of time, so that no one should be left to lament the others. Our household at this time consisted of my parents, Mary, Esther, Fred and myself; and old Sukie; and I might add Cousin Ridley, for he was always in and about the the place when not on the coach.

My Father was a Brighton coachmaster, and one of the very first men who drove a coach, properly so-called, between Brighton and London. He was an illiterate man, and yet no bumpkin; incapable of harbouring ill-will or suspecting an injury; stubbornly upright, gentle with

The Brighton of my Boyhood

all women, from his wife, "My tender soul," as he prettily called her, to any poor forlorn thing tramping it on the road ; and gentle with all animals and dependent things. It is true he could not write his name ; and yet when I remember how lovingly observant he was of every phase of the beauty through which he daily drove, and how simple and deeply rooted was his faith in God, and what a big tender heart he had for all His creatures, I cannot think he was greatly inferior for having lived before the days of compulsory education.

My Mother was really a fine specimen of exquisite though homely housewifery, and although at times of house-cleaning and such repairs, a little fussy and put about, she was really the most devoted wife and mother in England. Having received little or no education herself, she could ill sympathise with Mary's tastes, and was sometimes a little short with her on the subject. But then she grew inconsistently proud and pleased when the clergyman commended Mary's gifts to her, and wished he had such a tongue for French as she. Dear soul! Like many another at such moments, she quite forgot her sometime grudge against her daughter's aspirations,

The Brighton of my Boyhood

and said she thanked God she had always made an effort to give her children a good education, although she must say she had certainly thriven very well without one herself.

My eldest brother William was married and lived from home, and between him and Mary there was an interval of many years, during which two children had been born and had died; so that by the time that I, the youngest of all, came into this world, my father was already past middle age. Mary was my Father's clerk, and the right hand and head-piece of the whole house, a presence whose power we scarcely recognised until she once went away for a holiday to France, so quiet and untiring were the foresight and devotion which enabled the wheels of life to run so smoothly for us all. She went deep into her books in whatever little leisure her rigorous conscience granted her, and was always pleased to read aloud to us little ones, moving us to great wonder and delight with the marvellous doings of the Lady Britomart, and the Red Cross Knight, and the adventures of Christian, the Pilgrim. She read a great deal of French history in its proper tongue with Esther; but Esther was a pretty light-hearted girl,

The Brighton of my Boyhood

who would rather spend her leisure in walks among the hills, or visiting among friends, than in very much study.

My cousin Ridley, the hero of my boyhood, was only one of three of our kin whom my Father brought about him in Brighton, giving them regular work and a good wage in place of the dull life and insufficient earnings of the agricultural labourer of that period.

And then there was Sukie, in whom a mingle of natural shrewdness, obstinate ignorance, beautiful devotion, and peppery temper went to make up a servant the like of which you may seek long enough in these days.

But now enough of introduction. Come away with me into the last teens of this century, into old Brighton, and let us make straight for East Street, till we come upon my Father's office. Here it is, with the two large bowed-glass windows, all of small square panes, on either side the door, and with the pots of bright flowers in Esther's window above; and so, if you please, step up into the office, and through into the house behind, and let me make you better acquainted with the folk who live there.

Chapter 2

THE COACHMASTER

WHEN my Father was a Hampshire plough-boy, he often looked over the hedge and saw the coach go by from Winchester to Reading; and he thought of all things in this world it were best to be the driver of a coach.

Small wonder that he looked at the coach with longing and vague hope. On his side of the hedge, life was dull enough. He was always in the fields and had no schooling. His father could ill have spared

The Coachmaster

him for that, for the little lad's scant earnings made it possible to give the others a dinner of bacon once a week.

At an age when the children of gentlefolk were still at play in the nursery, he and his like must out with a clapper to scare

The Coachmaster

the rooks from the new-sown fields; or plod at the head of the plough, guiding the strong gentle horses, or crouch over the dull acres of fallow land, ridding them of stones from hedge to hedge.

And if the childhood was dreary and strenuous, the manhood was little better. To rise before day-break the long year through, to grow old and crippled before middle-manhood with the hard toil, poor fare and worse housing, this was the prospect for him and his like. This was the lot of his father before him, who had had the luck of getting the best wages to be earned in those parts. Upon this wage, eight shillings a week, he kept himself and wife and four children, living God knows how, in a two-roomed hovel, a picturesque little place with a mossy rotten thatch and bottle-glass windows, good for neither light nor air. For such there was neither change nor bettering, save from the clayey field to the tap-room of the " White Horse," until worn out by the long struggle with Mother Earth for bare existence, they came to claim a little space in her lap in which to lay their worn-out bodies.

On the other side the hedge a great road ran between two cities, either far away, and twice a week between the two

The Coachmaster

a coach sped by: a beautiful thing to the eyes of the little rustic, gay in yellow and black, and laden with a freight of happy souls, free as air and going whither they would. With the vanishing of the coach round the bend of the road, all dreams and possibilities died out, and life seemed dull and slow again as the plough he followed.

One day his master, a churlish fellow at all times, fell out with him about some trifling matter in most unjust fashion and dismissed him summarily from his service; whereupon he went home, kissed his mother, scraped the clay from his boots, and with a little bundle and a thick stick tramped for London. Hardships by the way and hardships in the great City he met in plenty, but he had been born and reared in want and was not to be easily disheartened.

I know little more of those early years in London than that his work lay always in or about stables, for he loved horses and was ever eager to fit himself for the position of coachman. Hard work, poor pay, a wretched lodging, and indifferent company—these were his lot; but a certain sturdy manhood in the Hampshire farm-lad, and the spur of an honest ambition,

The Coachmaster

kept him strong, and brought him clean, through that period of trial.

From stable-boy he became groom, and eventually coachman to Admiral H——. Now, indeed, was he come a long way on the road of his ambition, but the goal was yet to reach. It was all very well to take the young ladies on their purchasing rounds to the toy-shops and milliners, or to their dancing parties, or through the Park, but he looked ever more eagerly for the time when he should disentangle himself from the thronged and mazy London streets and drive his fine horses into the heart of the sweet country; and his pulse quickened at the thought of the rapid run along the free high roads in the pleasant company and talk of travellers.

In course of time, and to his great satisfaction, he entered the service of Mrs. Thrale, who had but recently gone to live in Brighton, and there can be little doubt that he must have driven Dr. Johnson in her carriage on the rare occasion of his visits to Brighton; but did he do so, he was quite unaware of the fact, and even ignorant of the name and fame of the ponderous philosopher.

"I won't say but what I *may* have driven him," he said thoughtfully, when,

The Coachmaster

in tremulous hope of a living touch with what had long since died into history for the outer world, I first questioned him upon the subject. "Let me see, did you say he was a physic-doctor?"

Perhaps I should here tell that my Father could neither write nor read to his dying day.

"I never had time for education," he once said naïvely, looking with huge admiration at a round-hand copy of my own doing. "You see, little Peter and Poll would never have tasted bacon if I had." His wages as a little lad had enabled his mother to give the other children a dish of this, the only meat they ever saw, one day in every week,

He spoke always with true liking and respect of Mrs. Thrale. "She was a kind lady," he said, "and a wonderful determined lady; she used to get up even in very cold weather by candlelight, aye, and make the young ladies get up too, and then all of them would run down to the beach and take their dip in the sea before dawn."

On leaving Mrs. Thrale's service, he was engaged as coach driver by Mr. Rudd, part owner of a well-known line of coaches running between London and Brighton,

The Coachmaster

and right glad he was to have made his way to this at last, although as yet the gay coach and the sturdy horses were none of his own. His careful, good driving, his punctuality, and his whole cheery personality soon won their way with the passengers, and he became one of the favourite coachmen on the road. It was, indeed, quite usual for passengers to inquire at the office when Hyde's coach would start, as they wished to travel by that, and would be willing to delay or hasten their departure, in order to do so. The Rudds were an odd family. The father was a man of nearly eighty years, with shaggy white hair and fierce eyes like an old lion, and one that could swear with any man in England. The sons were surly, ill-conditioned fellows enough, who greatly resented the fact of my father's popularity, and answered sometimes rudely enough — " Hyde's coach ? Hyde hasn't got a coach : he's our servant," and became at last so offensive to my Father's friends, and so tyrannical in their treatment of himself, that a little company of the most frequent passengers laid their heads together and decided that matters should go on in such a way no longer. The outcome of their discussion I shall delay telling a while, to relate a little

The Coachmaster

incident which shows, as I think, how good a servant the Rudds lost when my Father left their employ. One morning, several hours before the down coach should start, my Father, on going to report himself at the office in Fetter Lane, was informed curtly that the coach would not run that day. Neither then nor after could he win any explanation; he would sometimes say he suspected Mr. Watty, old Rudd's partner and his informant, had been drinking, or had had some serious quarrel with his partner in Brighton; but indeed he never properly understood the strange incident. He was told that if he touched the coach or horses that day, he would do so at the risk of instant dismissal. My Father was not one to be stayed if he knew a thing must be done. He went straightway to his friend, the proprietor of the "Old Bell" in Holborn, himself a coach-owner formerly, who in this dire extremity lent him an old coach which had stood unused for several years. Then together they managed to borrow four horses, a motley crew indeed: two lean bays from a job-master, a third with the proportions of a young cart-horse from a friendly butcher, the fourth being a jog-trot mare of venerable age, the pro-

The Coachmaster

perty of my Father's friend. After much brushing up and cleaning down the coach was ready to start, and my Father, making such excuse and explanation to the passengers as involved no blame on his employers, rattled away from the "Old Bell" with his unsightly and ill-matched four,

only half an hour behind the usual time. Old Rudd was much gratified by his perseverance in a good cause, and when he went up to town the next day, Mr. Watty probably recognising, after a good night's sleep, that my Father had helped to save the good name of the firm, said very abruptly,

"You were quite right to do what you did, Hyde, last night, quite right," and then changed the subject.

The Coachmaster

"I'd have done it, my boy," said my Father in after years, as he told me of the awkward handful he found in those four horses, "if I'd only been able to get four old bulls I'd have done it!" And I believe he would.

My Father had been married some years and was finding it hard enough to keep a wife and a growing group of youngsters on his wages from Rudd, when the little company of old passengers of earlier mention, clubbed together and lent him £1000 wherewith to set up coach and horses of his own, on condition that he would never lower his prices. Exceedingly wroth were the young Rudds at the proceeding, and determined promptly to reduce the price of seats on their own coaches, and caused bills announcing the fact to the travelling public to be printed. Old Rudd happening to meet his son carrying a bundle of them fresh from the printer's, seized them, and glancing hastily through the first, tore the whole lot across and threw them on the ground. "Damn you all!" he roared, kicking the fragments about the office. "It shall never be said I helped to ruin a man's family!" And so the matter ended, and they did not succeed in underselling my Father.

The Coachmaster

And now began my Father's happier fortunes, which indeed so grew and flourished that after no great interval he was able to repay the sum so generously loaned to him.

He had not forgotten the poor folk he had left behind in the little thatched Hampshire cottage so many years back ; and had from time to time sent thither all he could spare of his wages, by the hand of his friend the guard of the Winchester coach. By the same messenger he once sent a workbox and a cherry-coloured ribbon for little Poll : who soon brought them back again, for little Poll was dead of the fever ; which was a great sorrow for my Father. Since then the old mother and father had both died in one very hard winter, and of all of the little group he loved only two brothers were left, and as it had long been his wish to bring his kin about him, he hailed this rise in his fortunes as the fit occasion. So there appeared one day in Brighton brothers Peter and Jim ; and a little later, from the same parts, John Ridley, a nephew of my Mother and a bright good-looking lad, who had always been a favourite with my Father. All aglow with the pleasure of having his own kin with him again, my Father welcomed them with a heartiness

The Coachmaster

which a little confounded the grinning countrymen. He put them in a comfortable lodging, gave them regular work about his stable-yard, and started them at once with a higher wage than they had ever yet received.

This arrangement proved to be but little to my Father's advantage, and yet for many years he retained them in his employ, indeed as long as he had any work for them to do. They were dull fellows, and, as I fear, jealous of his better fortunes; Uncle Peter, especially, the eldest of the family, and a man of over fifty, was a thankless soul, and as obstinate as a mule. Down in Hampshire he had had the care of a great many farm horses, and for all my Father could say, he would not be persuaded to treat his far more delicate and valuable beasts in any other fashion than he had treated those, often with the worst results. At last the coachmaster, kindliest of men, could stand it no longer: Boxer, his favourite bay, was getting into thoroughly bad condition from over-feeding. In one of his rare but real rages he left the house and hurried round to the yard, while I, always glad of a peep at the stables, trotted at his side. He muttered to himself all the way about "the poor beasts,"

The Coachmaster

and "an ungrateful good-for-naught," and "he'd let him see who was master!" and the like. As we entered the yard the old yokel plodded up to us and he looked at

my Father with a twinkle in his small eyes. "Good mornin', Willum," he said, innocently chewing a straw. "Come to have a look at the beasts?" The coachmaster's face grew red as a winter sunset and he

The Coachmaster

said nothing; he looked terribly guilty. "Good morning t' ye, brother Peter," he said. "Yes, I've come to have a look at the beasts, if it won't be putting you out;" and a moment later he was in among them, calling them by their names, patting them, feeling their legs, and discussing them amicably enough with the wily old fellow. His face was clear of all anger now, "But · I think, brother Peter," he said, more than once, "there is such a thing as too much kindness towards beasts—more especially horses;" and then carelessly, with a wave of the hand towards the yard, "I must tell some of them fellows not to come meddling with your work, and letting the beasts eat their heads off!" At the stable door he felt in his pocket. "Well, lad, here's a crown for you and Jim, and keep an eye on the feeding, won't you?" he said, and so left, chuckling at his own wiliness, and well content that the hint had gone home along with the coin. I fear he was a mean old man, Uncle Peter. Sprightly told me he often made sport of my Father, in such clumsy fashion as was possible to him, behind his back; and certain it is that when the troubles came he was the first to leave the brother who had so long employed and cared for him.

The Coachmaster

Coaching at that time was a very different thing from what it became a few years later. Not so very long before, the best conveyance between London and Brighton was a "Flying Machine," which an advertisement of that date describes in this wise: "A new large Flying Chariot, with a box and four horses, to carry two passengers only, except three should desire to go together." This vehicle left Brighton or Charing Cross at six in the morning, to arrive at its journey's end at the somewhat indefinite hour "that evening," such journey, according to the advertisement, "to be performed (if God permit)." As Brighton grew more fashionable, and the dandies and beauties of the Court came down for an airing to the village by the sea, there appeared on the road Patent Coaches, and various other vehicles; but none of these reached the even moderate standard of convenience and comfort attained a few years later. When my Father started with his two-horse coaches in the very first years of this century, four and a half miles an hour was considered a respectable pace, and to do the distance between London and Brighton in twelve was all that would reasonably be desired. But then, to be sure, there was a

The Coachmaster

deal to be done beside the secondary business of getting from one place to another. For example, the down coach, whose passengers had already broken their fast at nine in Sutton, must needs always pull up at the "Tangier" on Banstead Downs, where coachmen and travellers drank a glass of its famous elderberry or other home-made wine, and gossiped a little with the pleasant soul who brought it out to them; then at Reigate there was a cave to be seen and a light lunch to be partaken of; and then, who, with any sense of civility, would have sought to evade the rustic hospitality of the little hostelry at Hand Cross, whose host always appeared as the coach drew up, in one hand a gallon bottle of gin, and in the other a wicker basket filled with thin slices of ginger-bread? And was there not the halt for dinner at Staplefield Common, where the celebrated rabbit pies and home-brewed ale of the hostess often induced the passengers and coachman to linger an hour and a half, or even two hours? And then there was the retailing of London news to the landlords of the wayside hostelries; and old Mrs. Loveday at the last Turnpike, who must always bring her little nosegay for Mr. Hyde; and,

The Coachmaster

indeed, at least a hundred and one hindrances of the pleasantest kind in the

world, which I think I may say were very seldom regretted or resented by that easygoing, unelectric generation.

By the year 1811 there were no less than

The Coachmaster

twenty-eight coaches running between London and Brighton, and the competition resulted in greatly increased comfort, punctuality and speed. My Father altered his ways like the rest, and never again drove less than four horses. Though there was now so large a choice of coaches, my Father was increasingly popular among travellers on that road. His coaches were always well-horsed, well-appointed, and his pace was excellent; but he would none of the dashing style or racing with other coaches, so popular among the showy "whips" of the day, and occasionally so disastrous to their passengers.

"The Alert" and "The Union" left our office at nine and eleven respectively, driven by my Father and Crosby; their twin coaches leaving the "Old Bell," Holborn, at the same hours, driven by my cousin Ridley and Merryman. My Father always prepared for his departure on the up-coach with the regularity of a clock. After breakfast he drew on his high boots, and with his neckerchief in his hand he went out into the kitchen. Now this neckerchief was as large as a fair-sized table-cloth, and the right folding of it could only be achieved upon a table: a clean deal table was here set apart for this purpose,

The Coachmaster

and as long as I can remember anything, I remember the folding of the kerchief in that appointed place.

Very uncongenial is the roar and racket of our great railway stations to one who remembers the pleasant bustle of our goings and comings in the old coaching days. Castle Square was the centre of the coaching life of Brighton. There were situated "The Blue," "The Red," "The Age," and other coach offices, and the running in and out of persons eager to secure good seats, the handling of luggage, the departure and arrival of coaches, and the crowd of ladies and gentlemen and other simpler folk who came to greet or bid farewell to friends, kept the place astir and humming from morning till evening. The departure of "The Age" brought together the largest number of gazers and loafers: and indeed that coach was a thing worth going a little way to look at, with its pole-chains of burnished steel, and its daintiest of ribbons and superb horses in silver-mounted harness, and horse-cloths embroidered with royal crowns in silver and gold.

My Father's coaches started from our office in East Street: at five minutes to nine he mounted his box, and satisfied himself that Varney had put a sufficient

The Coachmaster

number of great coats and capes under the seats for the protection of those unsuitably clothed in the case of inclement weather, looked to the comfortable settling of passengers in their appointed places, while the porters bestowed the last of the baggage, then he took his seat with the air of a man settling down to well loved work, and at the first stroke of the hour from the clock in the old Pavilion Tower, the ostlers whipped off the horse-cloths, my Father tightened the ribbons, raised his whip, and off they went.

And here I may say that my Father always drove out of Brighton with four bays, and Ridley out of London with four greys. A bay was ever my Father's favourite horse; Boxer and the Mare, the two oldest and most beloved of his horses, were both bays, and a pair of faithful sweethearts he said, and I believe he grew more partial to creatures of their colour every time he drove them. For a black horse he had no liking, indeed it was a kind of terror to him.

Of course there may be many of those who growl at the memory of that old fashion of travelling, but even they will grant you, unless they be wholly bent on saving time at the expense of life and

The Coachmaster

pleasure, that there was a certain charm in it, in each season of the year as it came round; and especially to those who made the down journey. Yes, I can give you my word, as that of a country creature shut up for many hours daily in the dingy office of an engraver in a desolate London street, that it was pleasant enough to leave the town in the early spring, of whose coming in a London square or a city court only a few smutty lilac bushes and a solitary plane-tree had given dubious promise; to rattle away through the streets and out into the roads where the bricks and mortar dwindled with every yard we covered, and the greening hawthorn hedges sprang up in their stead by the wayside, breaking out here and there into blackthorn with its million stars or the willow palm in silver and gold; while in the fields on the further side of the hedge the clumsy lambs sucked their mothers greedily, or made merry in their own inconsequent fashion; and we knew that a skylark must be singing overhead, if we could but hear him through the noise of the wheels; and all this in an air that grew momently lighter than laughter, and gladding as wine. Or later in the year, when all the world was deep in summer, and the dust we raised whitened

The Coachmaster

the leaves of the bramble, and dimmed the beauty of the dog-rose that garlanded the wayside in pink and white, and the air was sweet with stricken grass and buttercups, and hay-makers tilted back their shady battered hats the better to see and grin at us. Or later still, to enter a Sussex lane when the gnats were humming all about the honeysuckles, and children with tin cans were deep in every bramble-bush gathering blackberries, and the reapers in the fields bent over their work, sickle in hand, and had scarce a glance for us save when they stayed in their work to mop their tanned faces, so precious was every moment of the gorgeous golden afternoon. Or even much later, when the fields were bare and the roads hard and folks' noses were red, and they talked of fires and the woeful big price one must needs pay for them; and the hot elderberry wine at the Tangier tasted like nectar, and the crowd of sparrows flew out of the stout holly tree we passed on the road, the poor wretches finding little enough of food otherwhere in such hard season . . . . yes, they were all pleasant enough in their several ways, were the four seasons to the traveller of those days; provided he had a kindly heart and simple tastes.

The Coachmaster

I think, too, there was a special pleasure for those who rode on my Father's coach. He was out-and-out a good coachman, and by a good coachman I do not merely mean a man who keeps his horses to a fine pace

without harm to them or risk for his passengers. I mean your genial fellow who looks upon these last, not as so many fares, but as guests who must be kindly looked after, and, if need be, entertained ; and my father had ever that way with him. He had an intimate knowledge of the history of places along the road, and he gave it

The Coachmaster

interest in the manner of telling. He could tell you, so as to make you creep again, the story of that lone farmhouse over there, with its solitary inhabitant, and show you the exact spot where, forty years ago, a highway robbery was committed and the postillion shot. He could give you a very pretty and amusing account of the old post-chaise times and the early coaches and the "flying machines" and the crawling forerunners of such vehicles as his own. And he had an excellent store of fine old jokes, gathered in the course of many appreciative years passed on the road, and would often set his box-seat traveller laughing aloud with the telling.

"What's it all about?" somebody would ask, and then our friend on the box-seat retails it over his shoulder, and friend two delivers it to the rest of the company, and the fun and interest of it, as it goes the round, bring them all into kindly touch with one another like a glass of good wine.

Then, too, there were certain interesting persons who not infrequently visited Brighton, and who invariably travelled by my Father's coach on these occasions. Happy they who found themselves travelling with Emery, Russell, Mimic Matthews,

The Coachmaster

or Joe Munden—Munden "with the bunch of countenances, the bouquet of faces," the recollection of whose antic drolleries kept Charles Lamb so long awake on one occasion that he only fell asleep in the small hours fairly exhausted by a passion of laughter. Good company, these, on a coach journey, and I daresay considerate and unselfish fellow-travellers, like all your true Bohemians. It was with child-like pleasure my Father would tell us how each of these actors had at one time or another borrowed his huge box-coat with seven capes when figuring on the boards of the Brighton Theatre.

It was not unusual for "The Alert" or "Union" to carry a very different order of passengers. My Father had always a tender heart for trampers, and would always give them a lift if he could without reasonable inconvenience to his other passengers. One day I was sitting by his side (it was out of the season and the coach was very empty), and he pointed to a man trudging along wearily, with a basket of tools under his arm.

"Now, that fellow thinks himself Mr. Walker," said he, "but I think we must turn him into Mr. Rider;" and a minute later we pulled up.

The Coachmaster

"But I haven't got any money," said the man, raising a tired, sweaty face.

"Get up with you get up with you, for God's sake, and don't stand there talking about money!" cried my Father; and when the fellow, red with pleasure, had scrambled up, there began a quaint enough conversation, my Father's part being purely catechetical.

"Married?" asked my Father, looking over his shoulder at his passenger.

"Yes."

"Good woman?"

"Yes."

"Got work?"

"No."

"Don't drink?"

"No."

On our arriving at the next hostelry, where we changed horses and my Father's meal awaited him, he said to the young man, "Now, lad, you must run into that little parlour; you'll find some capital beef and lettuce and a mug of ale there: get along and make the best of your time." And he did, and I ate, too, while my Father chatted with the landlord and contented himself with a bit of bread and cheese.

We landed the poor fellow in London,

The Coachmaster

and I saw my Father slip a coin into his hand at parting.

"Good-bye, lad," said he, clapping the rather dazed countryman on the shoulder. "Stick to the thought of your wife and babbies, and be shy of the drink, and keep a good heart" In every such case I think he saw himself again, the poor Hampshire farm-lad tramping his way to London to make his fortune.

Which little incident, and indeed all my Father's way with needy and helpless folk, goes to persuade me how good it is for a man that would live kindly and Christianly among men, to have once been poor. If you have heard the pit-pat of the wolf coming up your garden path, and his sniffing at the very keyhole, you will, when the time comes, be the very first to go knight-erranting after the merciless beast on behalf of a fellow-creature. The man born to property and power, for all his admirable intentions and philanthropic tendency, has had too many cushions betwixt him and life to realise its instant and most poignant needs. It is the man that has been at such close grips with want, whose heart is ever at the beck and call of misery. He leaves that other conscientiously scheming for the future welfare

The Coachmaster

of the masses, and hurries away with all that he has of purse and pity to the help of the individual sorrow. And so it seems to me, that if more among us had tramped on foot to our better fortunes, we should seldomer pass a wayfarer in our well-horsed respectability, but should pull up and give him a lift on his road and a kind "God speed" at parting.

It was not often that my Father's coach carried an unwelcome passenger, for he had a big undiscriminating heart that deemed the vast majority of people kind and pleasant, because, in truth, he was himself kind and pleasant to everybody. But one day, just before the coach should start, my Father came down the office steps in a great state and with a very red face.

"Look there, boy," he said, gripping my arm, as I stood at the head of the off leader, and he pointed, or rather shook his fist, at a gentleman on the box-seat. "Look at that old fellow up there on the box-seat," he cried, with an angry tremor in his voice; "he will come, and *I* don't want him, and *he* knows I don't want him, too! I'd as soon have the devil sitting 'long side of me as him!" And he climbed to the box with indignation and disgust writ large on his whole person and bearing. I ran

The Coachmaster

into the booking-office and asked of Mary the name of the offender, and learned he was a well-known Informers' Magistrate.

The informers were people who rode on or spied about coaches, earning a certain sum for every reported case of overloading: did a coachman suffer but one person more than his correct number to ride ever so short a distance, he was liable to be fined £5. This man, the head of an ancient family of our county, was known to have many of these creatures at work up and down the road; and in every instance that the case was tried before him, the informer's word was taken before that of the coachman, often to the real hurt of the latter. Several of my Father's friends on the road had suffered most harshly and unjustly at the hands of the mean, cantankerous old squire, and hence his honest aversion to his company.

The coachmasters of that time were for the most part a deep-drinking, hard-swearing set of men, but in this respect my Father differed delightfully from them. For all his love of good comradeship, he was the most abstemious soul in the world, and I never in my life, save once, knew him to swear. It was on one occasion when there had come to his ears a tale of

The Coachmaster

great cruelty, cruelty of a man to a child, if I remember rightly. As he listened his face grew very red, and then he brought his fist with a great thud on the table. "Damn his heart, he ought to be shot!" he roared, with the tears of rage and pity in his eyes.

If ever God made a man quite incapable of remembering personal injury or unkindness, or of paying back the like with aught but kindliness, it was my Father. On one occasion as he was leaving his coach at the "Old Bell," he was arrested by a couple of bailiffs. Upon his demanding indignantly what was their business with him, they replied that it was on account of a little bill that had been too long owing, and that it were wiser to come along quietly.

"I don't understand you—I don't know what you are talking about—I owe no one a penny as far as I know!" said my Father in a great rage, and indeed he was scrupulous to a nicety about such things.

"I'm very sorry, sir," said one of the bailiffs, "but if you like we can call a coach and you can come along quietly enough and no one will be the wiser."

"Coach, indeed!" cried my Father. "I'll ride in no coach! If I have to go I'll go openly! Come along, sir, come

The Coachmaster

along with you!" And the indignant old man marched off between the two to the office of him who had issued the writ, a certain lawyer in Fleet Street. Here my Father, in a great fluster and higher choler, demanded an explanation, and the lawyer had to tell him that a mistake had been made, and that he saw now that the writ was issued against a Mr. Hythe, not Mr. Hyde, the former being also a coachmaster. And he thereupon tendered my Father an awkward apology, which immediately dispelled his indignation.

Telling us of the incident next day, he concluded by saying, "Ah, that lawyer's an uncommon good fellow: he spoke me so civilly and nicely—yes, a very good fellow indeed."

"And so he need be," broke in Mary, tartly; she had felt the offence to her Father far more painfully than he himself; "I should say he could not be *too* nice, after making so shameful a blunder!" And my Mother too cried out on the man for his scandalous carelessness.

"Never mind, never mind," said my Father. "He's a good fellow, a very good fellow indeed. I must take him up a basket of fresh fish to-morrow."

My Father had one strange delusion;

The Coachmaster

he often said, and heartily believed, that he had never met with anything but love and kindness all his life: and neither argument nor laughter could ever shake him in his stubbornly happy faith.

"Why, you old stupid," said my Mother more than once, half-peevish, half-amused, "won't you ever remember? There's that old scoundrel, Tommy Larkins, borrowed £50 of you, and never pays a penny of it though he drives his own coaches now; and there's that young rogue, young Penfold, that robbed you when you were so ill—he and his folks have been living on you, time out of mind." And, indeed, there were not a few memories of ingratitude and mean action towards this simple generous soul stored away in my Mother's loyal heart, and bitter enough upon her tongue at times. But her words made less impression upon him than water may upon the duck's back.

"Aye, mother, how you do talk, love!" he would interrupt her, shaking his head. "Jack Penfold a rogue indeed! little Jackanapes, I used to call him," with a pleasant laugh at old memories. "Why, my tender soul, I've known his father, and mother too for that matter, this forty year come Michaelmas, nicest people as ever

The Coachmaster

breathed—and him when he was a little chap no higher than that!"

That was an argument not to be answered, according to his way of thinking.

As my Father advanced in years, trouble came thick and thicker about him. My sister Esther died and my brother Edward, and then my cousin Ridley began his unworthy behaviour. He was the handsomest man I have ever seen, and the hero and pattern of my boyhood. For years he served my Father well and honestly, but when I was growing into a big lad, I noticed that people pulled long faces when they spoke of him; and one day my Mother said before me, " If folks live as wild and loose as Ridley they must expect to get into trouble." I felt very uncomfortable and wretched, for I was still fond of him: and then I began to notice a change in his bearing. He was often short and impatient with me, who once had been so kind and had taught me boat-building and the cutting of whistle-pipes, and a hundred other contrivances for making childhood the goldenest age of all. Worse than that, I heard him more than once speak in an uncivil and hurtful way to my Father; this the kind old man took sorely to heart, for

The Coachmaster

he loved Ridley and had lifted him out of his dull labouring life, and had taught him his honourable and more remunerative business, and he treated him ever as an elder son. I mind well how one day about that time, my Father came home and told us of his meeting with Ridley on the road, who was driving the four greys, and how he had noticed his fidgety and impatient handling of reins and whip.

"Poor Ridley! poor lad!" said he, sadly and kindly; "he's not at peace with himself, and his poor beasts have to suffer for it."

A few years later Ridley, who by that time had gone sadly wrong, started an opposition coach to my Father, and very sore and aggrieved we all felt about the matter. But my Father, after the first shock and astonishment, met Ridley and was by him easily soothed and persuaded to see the matter from his point of view, and came home saying, "Ah, I thought the poor fellow meant nothing wrong by us. I thought I knew the dear lad!" which remark caused my Mother to laugh and cry at the same time; for, with the best heart in the world, she did not share his benevolent short-sightedness.

It was all of a piece with his deep

The Coachmaster

conviction that he had never received anything but love and kindness all his life. He was indeed, and never coachman more, beloved and respected by his many old passengers, and the landlords, ostlers, and toll-keepers all along the road; but his kind heart and generosity were well known, and not only honestly appreciated, but traded upon. At certain breaks in the journey he was perfectly surrounded by old women with little offerings, all of which he received with delight and paid for three-fold.

"There's old Mother Loveday at the Toll," he would say to us at home, "and poor old Mrs. Blaker at Horley, and many another; they never fail to bring me their little nosegay or fresh lettuce just cut, or a leaf of raspberries. Kind old souls! I must take them up some fine fresh fish to-morrow!"

"Bless the man!" said my mother, sometimes laughing, sometimes vexed, "hasn't he got any eyes to see what the old creatures are after all the time?"

I had been out in the world some time when my Father's lawsuit came on. In all the years he had been on the road, and he was now an old man, he had never had an accident; but now it came. He had himself no part in it, the coach being driven by

The Coachmaster

my brother at the time, neither was there loss of life to passenger or horse. A lady, the single passenger at the time of its happening, suffered, it was said, such a shock to her nerves, that her friends thought it right to demand £500 damages. My Father, to whom, for all his thriving business, such a sum was a great consideration, resisted so large a claim by persuasion of my Mother and others. The claim was immediately doubled, and a lawsuit ensued in which he lost his case. The payment of this sum was a terrible pull on his purse, but the accident itself, the first incident to cast a shadow on his long coaching career, was by far the heavier trouble to him, and it aged him sadly.

There was a witness called in for my Father during that lawsuit whom I remember well. He was a brown brawny fisherman, called Speedwell Jasper, and he was only one of the many poor folk, who loved and honoured the Coachmaster.

"Will you swear to this?" asked the lawyer, referring to some point in the case.

"Swear to it? I sh'd think I would! I'd swear to anything for old Master Hyde," replied this devotedly unreliable witness.

I was at this time living in London,

The Coachmaster

apprenticed to an engraver, and it was always my endeavour to run round to the "Old Bell" in the evenings that my

Father's coach came in. Something misgave me sadly when I noted this sudden change at the time of the lawsuit, though, to be sure, the manner was as cheery, and the dear heart as kindly as ever. His was a nature incapable of taking injury from trouble; it could wound him, but it could not harden or sour him.

The Coachmaster

Misfortune had not yet had her will with him. Shortly after the termination of the lawsuit, glanders broke out in his stables. Horse after horse went down with it, and many that were purchased to fill their places failed after a little while with the same disease, for all the care and precaution that was taken; the murrain was in the very harness. This matter of the horses was a ruinous business; and I know how great the Coachmaster's suffering must have been in spite of his brave heart; for his beasts were very dear to him, and he knew the ways of each one, and took ever a loving pride in their sound condition and pretty show.

I came as usual on one of those evenings in the courtyard of the "Old Bell" to see him and to hear all news, and to send greetings home.

"Well, Father," I said cheerily, though I was like to have cried at sight of the careworn face, " all well at home ? "

" Yes, my boy, yes, thank God. Mother and Mary all well," he said, folding and unfolding his box-coat, with hands that visibly trembled.

" Things generally going on all right—I mean as well as we can hope for ? "

" Very well," he replied slowly, still busy

The Coachmaster

with the coat, "very well indeed, my boy. I left Boxer and the mare to be shot this morning," he added hurriedly, and burst into tears. They were the two horses he loved above all the rest—the two sweethearts as he called them—and they were his best horses for all that they were some of the oldest too.

A few days later, speaking to me of his two favourites—of their gentleness, their readiness for work, their long years of service seemingly so harshly repaid by that strange death—he added, " But I've been thinking, boy, more and more, that it's wrong to fret; for if the Almighty hadn't given me horses, I couldn't have lost them, could I ? "

Loss followed on loss, and trouble on trouble. The first railway between London and Brighton was opened, and that railroad was cut right through the livelihoods of many families, our own among many others. Things could hardly have happened less happily for our fortunes. My Father had recently sold the interest of the coaches to a friend, the proprietor of the " Old Bell," but had not received the purchase money : nor did he ever get it either, for his friend himself suffered so severely by the coming of the

The Coachmaster

railway that my Father could not find it in his heart to claim it.

My Father finding himself in a sorry plight indeed, felt in honour bound to call a meeting of his creditors; there were not many of them, and they were chiefly farmers and corn-merchants, from Lewes or thereabouts. So they came on a sultry August afternoon, and met together in the parlour of the "Old Ship." My Father was then too ailing to attend; and it appeared that when these worthies were all assembled they were quite at a loss as to what they should do. One can picture them, I think, after their first interchange of nods and laconic rustic greetings, eyeing one another furtively, or gazing round the room at the engraving of his Majesty George IV. in coronation robes, and the coloured print of "The Age" coach, driven by the Hon. S. J——; and then the heroic attempt of some one to make conversation on the subject of the late swine-fever, or the prospect of the harvest; and the sudden silences, when the same man started a gentle whistle to keep his spirits up, and everybody waited for some one to begin.

At last a huge bull-necked corn-merchant from Lewes stood up and said,

The Coachmaster

"Well, gentlemen, I don't know if you know why we've come here; I'm sure I don't know. Speaking for myself, and no man can do more, and I'm sure as you'll all agree with me, Mr. Hyde has paid up regular as clock-work till these blessed losses of late, and I'm sure I wish he may yet come and have many a sack of oats off me, for I know he'll pay the first moment he's got it to pay with; and I don't think there's a man here but wishes him well through these hard times." The honest fellow mopped his forehead with his red cotton handkerchief, for he was not accustomed to speak so long at a time. And here a husky young farmer blurted out that he hoped that Mr. Hyde would come to him if he wanted a horse at any time; for he'd never had pleasanter dealings with any man than with Mr. Hyde, and as to paying, why everybody knew that Mr. Hyde would pay when he could, and for his part his little bill should bide a good time for such a kind old gentleman as Mr. Hyde. And there he left off, very red and surprised at his own eloquence; and the company bumped the table with their fists as they were used to do after the speeches at a tenants' dinner: and one after another remarked that that was just their way of

The Coachmaster

feeling, and why on earth they'd even come there they couldn't say. So they called for some ale and cider, and betook themselves to their carts, or mounted their cobs and jogged leisurely home on the hot white roads.

My Father was sitting at tea in the little parlour behind our office in East Street, glancing every now and again at a piece of paper lying by his plate, full of the figures Mary had been totting up for him, when in came the Lewes corn-merchant.

"Hullo! old friend, what's all this?" cried the kindly giant in a voice that went well with his size. "Calling your creditors indeed! Never heard of such a thing in a man of *your* respectability! And don't you know as all of us to a man 'ud be proud to serve you with goods as long as you want 'em? and dang the payment till times are good again!"

My Father looked up at him with open eyes and mouth, then he stretched out his hand to him and tried to speak his thanks.

"I'm sure we hardly know how to thank you," said my sister Mary, coming forward and putting her right hand in the good fellow's, and her left on my Father's shoulder, "but we do thank you, Mr. Roffey, and the other gentlemen too, very truly indeed."

The Coachmaster

And she added with a tremor in her voice, " I cannot tell you how precious the kindness of friends is to my dear Father in this time of loss and sorrow." It was well that Mary came to the rescue in that manner, for my Father, and no shame to him, had laid his head on his arms and was crying like a child. And that was how it came about that the Coachmaster never went bankrupt.

Of course my Father felt it now wrong, nay impossible, to attempt to maintain his old business. The office was closed, and my parents betook themselves and the little household gods that had kept in their niches so many a long year, to a small house in Ship Street, with Mary their loving housekeeper, and a young man as boarder, whose weekly payments helped a little towards the rent; and there they lived simply enough on the little sum my Father had contrived to save out of the wreck of his trebly reduced earnings. I, who was now a married man, went down to see them in the new home as soon as I could spare money for the journey. I found my dear old Father looking much older than when I had last seen him, walking with a stick among the flowers in his little walled garden; and this was the first

The Coachmaster

garden he had ever had. He was tenderly glad to see me, and we had much to say to one another. I can remember, it seems to me, every word he said, as if it were but yesterday; and I hope my heart may keep them in evergreen memory. Just before we entered the house, he laid his hand on my arm and said slowly, " Look here, my boy, when first I closed the office and left the old place where all you little ones were born and some of you died, and came here, I thought my heart was broke; I was full of wicked, ungrateful thoughts. And now see how good the Almighty has been to me! Here's this young man come as a boarder, and helps us pay our way, and I've come to love him like a son almost, now that my boys must all be out and away from me; and there's Mary so good to me, and keeps the place so bright, and the little garden and all—my boy" he said, solemnly stopping in his walk, and gripping my arm so tight that I almost cried out, "when I walk about this little garden I have such thoughts—such thoughts as I wouldn't exchange for thousands!" and the big tears fell as he spoke.

Blessed thoughts they must indeed have been, dear old man, to keep your heart so patient and brave under all its trial!

The Coachmaster

The strain of the last few months had been very great on my Mother, and she had now sunk into a condition of querulous childishness, sad enough to see and live with; all the sadder, I think, because she had been in the past such a bright, busy soul, sharp at times in temper, but devoted indeed, and as fond of fun as any of us, in due season.

As I sat with my Father that afternoon, telling him about my wife and little child, and the little home I had made by dint of such hard work, my Mother broke out at intervals into peevish railing against him; and I do not forget his patient way with her. Every now and again came Mary and reprimanded her as if she were a child: "Mother, Mother dear, you mustn't say such things to dear Father, who is always so good to you."

His sunny unselfish nature found even a little fun where others feared he would find only pain and vexation.

"O my boy," he said to me that day, after one of her railing fits, "this is nothing to what she says sometimes, bless her! You should hear her then; it's as good as a bull-bait!" And he laughed heartily. "As good as a bull-bait, ain't it, Mother dear?" he repeated, taking her hand on

The Coachmaster

his knee, and gently patting it and nodding his head at her. She smiled and nodded in return; and I laughed too, with the tears in my eyes.

Not many months after my return to London, I received a sudden summons from Mary, saying that Father was very ill and begging me to come at once. It came late one evening, and though I went out at once in anxious haste, both the last train and the last coach had gone. Then I made my way to the Elephant and Castle in the hope of finding some carrier's cart that would be making the journey to Brighton. I shall never forget the kindness shown me there and all along the road for my Father's sake.

"I am old Mr. Hyde's son," I said, "and he is very ill: can you help me to get down to Brighton?" They did help me, and with all possible speed packed me off in a carrier's cart.

"Please sir," said an ostler, a poor disreputable-looking creature, just before I got into the cart, "take my love to Mr. Hyde and say as I hope he will soon be well again. Don't forget now, say Jimmy Hunt sends his love, will you?" Another fellow said, "I can't bear to think as he's ill and sufferin'; there never wern't such a

The Coachmaster

kind heart as his, and there's not like to be again. Why I do believe if he'd seen a worm in the road he'd have pulled to one side rather than go over it."

"Vat's the use of talkin'!" broke in a gruff old cabby in a many-caped coat, "Mr. Hyde's a right 'un, he is, and that's about it." As the cart moved off the ostler came and put his head under the tilt, "Don't forget to say that Jimmy Hunt sent his best love, sir, please sir," he said; and away we went.

A poor woman with a terrible toothache was my only travelling companion; I did what I could for her comfort, poor soul, wrapping her in my rug, and making a pillow of my small bag; and then I was left alone with grave thoughts of my Father, with whom along this very road I had travelled so happily, and so many times, and who, as I knew in my heart, would never travel along this road any more.

Whenever we stopped to change horses the driver told my errand, and all the folk came round me with inquiries and messages and expressions of sympathy. It is like a nightmare to remember those seemingly interminable delays, and the enforced shaking of hands all round, because I was

The Coachmaster

Mr. Hyde's son, and the movement of lanterns and the scrambling back to my place among the luggage, with my heart full of dread that I should be too late; and the moaning of the poor soul with the toothache. I know in truth, and I knew then, for all that the time seemed so long, there was not one unnecessary delay, and that both man and beasts did their very best for me.

I found my Father somewhat better than he had been at the time of Mary's summons, and weak as he was, he smiled cheerily on seeing me.

"I'm delighted to see you, boy," he said, "but I hope you didn't come on purpose to see me, did you? You've got a wife and little one to think of now, you know!" I was with him for two days, and he was very quietly happy. He seemed glad to speak of the old days, and the old coach road, and of some of the dear ones who had died long ago.

"If it pleased the Almighty," he said several times, "to let me get well for a little time, why that'd be all right; for He's been very good to me and so's every one: I've had nothing but love and kindness shown me all my life; but if He don't want me to get well, I'm not a bit afraid

The Coachmaster

to die, boy," he said in his hearty old way, "not a bit, not a bit."

He bade me a very tender farewell when my work compelled me to return to London, and I never saw him again.

The night after I left him he said to Mary, " Now my dearie, I'm feeling quite tired and I'm going to have a good three hours' sleep." It was then ten o'clock, and about one, the loving watcher knew that the deep sleep of exhaustion had drifted into the deepest sleep of all.

Chapter 3
Miss Patten's School

I WAS, as I think I have otherwhere said, the youngest of our family, and for that reason, rather than for any extraordinary merits of my own, was a person of no little importance in our simple world. Mary, in her wise fashion, saw that I ran a fair chance of becoming a spoiled child, a mother's child, and a home bird, at an age when hale lads should begin to rough-and-tumble it with other children; and so, greatly against the dictates of her own and my Mother's indulgent hearts, they decided that I should be sent away from home to

Miss Patten's School

a school where I should meet with other children and receive such tuition as was suitable for my tender age; for I was but six years old. If Mary had been allowed her own way she would have frankly told me the result of the family council, and was fully prepared to dry my tears and soothe my tremors. But my Mother, partly because her tender heart misgave her at the prospect of the inevitable scene of heartbreak and fuss, partly because she thought to make the break with my little home-world easier for me, dissuaded her from her sensible wish and drew her into the little conspiracy, the story of which I will here tell.

One bright morning my Mother nodded knowingly at me across the breakfast-table and said, "Mary and I are going to drive over to Henfield to see Miss Patten, and if a certain young gentleman is very, very good, he shall go too."

At this distance of time I cannot remember what was my precise plan of mischief for that day, but whatever it might have been I quickly abandoned it, and had a mind to be very good indeed. For the memory of a former visit to Miss Patten, and of her strawberry garden, and a sip of cowslip wine was still fragrant with me. Accordingly, about ten o'clock, Mary put

Miss Patten's School

me on a clean frill, and polished up my face, and we set out for a ten-mile drive in the gig.

When we drew up at Miss Patten's gate her day scholars (for she kept the village school) were just coming out of school, and they hung about with their slates and satchels to see us dismount. I remember congratulating myself, poor imp, that I was not old enough to go to school yet.

Miss Patten was very kind and nice. She patted my head, said I was quite a little man, and gave me a thick wedge of cake. Then she brought out cowslip wine and biscuits for my Mother and Mary, and they talked about my Father's health, and the weather, and the grand doings at the Pavilion, and then Miss Patten looked meaningly at me and said,

"I think little pitchers might run out into the garden, if you don't object, ma'am."

"That would be nice," said my Mother. "Run along and play, Harry, but be sure you don't touch anything."

With the tempting memory of the strawberry garden clear in my mind, I could not help but wish that Miss Patten would be more explicit in her reply. "Bless him, I'm sure he's welcome," left me with a dis-

Miss Patten's School

appointing uncertainty as to what I might or might not do.

I strolled up and down the narrow mossy paths, with longing eyes for the many fruit-bushes, and occasionally scrambled up the fence to spy into the pig-stye next door. After about half an hour I grew weary of this severe discipline and the midday heat, and re-entered the house. Coming out of the sunlight into the cool, dark parlour I could at first see nothing very plainly, but I could just perceive that the room was empty. I went down the stone passage, and seeing a door ajar, tapped, and went into the kitchen. Miss Patten, in a white apron, stood at the table with her arms deep in a pan of dough.

"Well, little man," she said, smiling, "what may you want?"

"Please, where's Mother and Mary?" I asked, and looked all round the little kitchen.

"Where's Mother and Mary?" repeated Miss Patten. "Oh—why—they've just gone out for a little walk, I expect."

"Will they come back soon?" I asked, tremulously, for I was rather shy of being left alone with the bright little woman.

"O yes, I daresay," she said. "I say, I wonder if a little boy called Harry would

Miss Patten's School

like to go and get some brandy-balls with this?" and she produced a penny from the depths of her pocket and handed it to me with a little bit of dough sticking to it.

After the purchase of brandy-balls I whiled away more time in the garden, returning at intervals to the cool parlour, with the light coming green through the creeper leaves round the window; but I was still unable to find my Mother and sister.

At last Miss Patten joined me in the garden. She came towards me beaming, and I made sure she had come to tell me they had returned.

"I wonder how you would like to pay me a little visit, Harry," she said; "to stop in the house, I mean, and sleep in such a dear, ducky little bed!"

"I don't know—thank you. I think I should like it very much if Mother——"

"Well, now—O my! isn't it a treat?—you are going to make me a little visit, and have such a lot of nice little girls and boys to play with, and——"

"And Mary and Mother'll be here too?" I broke in.

"O well, yes, I expect so," she said, flicking some flour off her gown. "But we'll see, we'll see."

Miss Patten's School

"Please, ma'am," I said, with my poor little heart beating very fast indeed, "am I to do lessons on this little visit?"

"Just a few, *nice* ones," she said, kindly, squeezing my hand as it lay in hers.

"Sums?" I ventured, with a ghastly sinking.

"Yes, yes," she said, smiling in the belief that she had lighted on my favourite study.

"I wish Mother and Mary would be quick and come," I said, after a melancholy pause.

Miss Patten stopped before a bush of white roses and began pulling off the dead ones.

"Well, they *will* come soon, dear," she said; "in a few days, you know—O yes, quite soon, just to see how you and I are getting on."

"In a few days," I stammered. "Not now? Not to-day?" and I burst into tears.

I was bitterly unhappy, wounded and hurt as only a child, a helpless dependent thing, can be. My Mother and Mary had tricked me, deliberately trapped me into this place, and had gone away and left me without one kiss or word of good-bye. Miss Patten, whom up to this time I had

Miss Patten's School

regarded as a kind lady attached to a Paradise of strawberry beds, became suddenly transformed into a terrible being, a schoolmistress in whose grasp I was left a helpless victim, a person who would pretend to take my Mother's place, who would wash and dress me, and make me do sums. I cried, in spite of all her efforts to pacify me, until dinner-time, and then could not eat for sheer misery. If I had a favourite dish at that period it was gooseberry pudding; there was one for dinner that day; but when I tried with my tears running into my plate to eat a little piece, it tasted quite different, and I wondered how I had ever liked it. I noticed, too, that the spoons and forks were dull and smeary, and entirely lacked the brightness that made our simple table at home so pleasant—the table in which my Mother took such pride. My heart swelled again on observing this, and my bitter tears welled up afresh at the memory of the home that seemed so cruelly, irretrievably lost to me.

Through all that choking meal, and the long afternoon, and in the evening when I went to bed, Miss Patten was very kind to me; but I found no comfort. Whenever she observed my trembling lips, or

Miss Patten's School

any undue use of my pocket-handkerchief, she said: "O my! look here, 'here's a pretty!" showing me generally something which I did not consider in the least pretty, while I resented the remark as being only suitable for use in conversation with infants in arms. Sometimes she varied it with, "Come, come, this will never do, we must stop crying soon, or your eyes and your nose will be red as a rose!" in a tone of aggressive cheerfulness.

Weeping I went to bed, and awoke in the morning tired and unrefreshed, and miserably shy at the thought of facing the other children and Miss Patten. This day was no brighter than the day before. My tears obliterated my sums before I could prove them, and dropped on the boiled mutton I could not swallow at dinner-time; and so it went on for three days and nights, while I felt myself the forlornest, forsakenest little creature upon earth.

On Thursday afternoon (I had come on the Monday—Black Monday for me!) I was plodding hopelessly through the three-times table, when Miss Patten's niece, who came in to do the housework, appeared in the schoolroom-doorway, and said that some one had called to see Master Hyde. Quite forgetful of school proprieties, I

Miss Patten's School

scrambled off the form and heard the astonished Miss Patten giving me her

formal leave to depart as I ran into the parlour.

Miss Patten's School

There in the cool green room stood my cousin Ridley. He was a young man of three-and-twenty, and I a child of six, but we were fast friends, and he was my big hero. He lifted me on to his knee and patted my head.

"O Ridley!" I said, and laid my head against his waistcoat.

"Well, boy, how are you? I thought I must just come and see you, you know. Place don't seem the same," he said, gently pulling my ear, "without young mischief teasing the life out of us."

I don't think I said anything, but clung to him with a rapture touched with despair. Here was one precious living bit of home that had not forgotten all about me, and he would soon be going and leaving me alone in the strange place with the dull forks and spoons, and the three-times table, and the lady who was not a bit like Mother or Mary. My cousin turned my face up to his, and I remember that he looked concerned.

"Come, tell us how you like being here, Harry," he said; but I could not, partly because I was afraid Miss Patten would hear, and partly because of the lump in my throat.

"Don't like being here at all, p'raps?

Miss Patten's School

he said, or rathered whispered. I nodded, and the tears welled up into my eyes.

"Do they bully you, or whip you? Tell me why you don't like it, Harry," he said gently.

I struggled to find voice.

"Because, because—I can't tie my shoestrings!" I broke out, and cried bitterly upon his shoulder. I believe Ridley cried too: at all events he did not speak for several seconds, and then said huskily, but with great determination, "Well, that settles it." He wiped my eyes and smoothed my hair, and bade me ask Miss Patten to come and see him as he was going to take me home.

She was very kind, and understood the situation at once: indeed I think she was rather glad to be rid of the responsibility of a boarder who ate nothing, and cried himself to sleep every night. O, I thought she was a nice dear lady, and the scholars were nice children, and the parlour was so cool and pleasant, as she arranged my crumpled frill, and washed my tearful face preparatory to departure. I kissed her with a right good will, and assured her I should come back again quite soon—with Mother and Mary, and so set forth holding Ridley's left hand, while in his right he

Miss Patten's School

carried the small bundle which contained my entire wardrobe.

Was there ever on this earth, for either boy or girl, was there *ever* such a home-going as that, so utterly, ridiculously, perfectly happy? I think not. I skipped, I sang, I ran all round Ridley. I gathered whole armfuls of wildflowers, and only laughed when the nettles stung me; and I ate an enormous chunk of gingerbread which he brought out of his pocket, for my usual appetite had returned with my happiness.

We really had a lovely time. Sometimes Ridley carried me on his shoulder to rest my dusty little feet: (the shoestrings constantly came untied, but somehow that did not distress me at all). He cut me wands from the hedge and made such fine whistle-pipes, and several times we rested under a tree and had furious games with head-choppers.

One remark of mine caused my cousin great merriment. An old lady had once said in my hearing, thinking, I suppose, to please my mother, " So this is little Henry, your youngest, ma'am? Ah, he's the flower of the flock!" I remembered this for some reason or another as we tramped along the dusty road, and I gave a little

Miss Patten's School

jump for joy as I called to mind that Ridley too was the youngest of his family.

"O Ridley," I said, "isn't it nice that both you and me are the flower of the flock!"

My cousin was mightily tickled at this; indeed he rolled on the grass to enjoy his laugh the more thoroughly, and I promptly seized that opportunity to run off with his hat. And so we had altogether the merriest time in the world.

Mother and Mary nearly smothered me with hugs when I arrived hot, dusty, and rapturously happy, and just in time for tea; and when my Father came in on the afternoon coach, my joy was indeed complete.

Long afterwards I learned that Miss Patten, distressed at my grief and homesickness, had sent word of it to my Mother. The matter was discussed in full family conclave, and Ridley spoke up and said,

"I believe I know Harry as well as any of you, and I know this, that if you don't have him back he'll die; he's just the kind to die of fretting."

Both my Mother and Mary were by that time only too inclined to think with him, and so they bade him go and see for himself how matters stood with me and to act then as he thought best.

Miss Patten's School

"I shall have his little sheets aired and the bed made; so remember, it's all ready for him," said my Mother; "I mean in case—in fact, for my part, I should *like* to see the child home again; but of course, as Mary says, we must be reasonable."

And so Ridley came and saw and brought me back to home and happiness.

Our Gentleman Boarder — Chapter

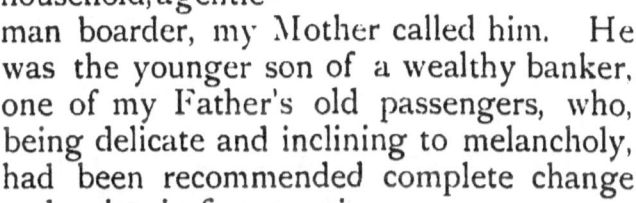

THERE came a day of great excitement and bustle in our quiet house. The afternoon coach was to bring an addition to our household, a gentleman boarder, my Mother called him. He was the younger son of a wealthy banker, one of my Father's old passengers, who, being delicate and inclining to melancholy, had been recommended complete change and quiet, in fine sea air.

Before that day was half over we two boys were tired of the preparations made for him, and weary of being bidden, "Be careful, be careful, don't put your elbows on that white cover," and "Don't go in there with your dirty shoes," and "You'll have to play more quietly when the poor

Our Gentleman Boarder

young gentleman is here ; " and at last, hot as it was, Fred strolled sulkily down to the beach. But I, having been already washed, brushed, and befrilled, and put into my best breeches, was bidden stay at home, as no one would have time to put me straight again later. I had on white nankeen trousers which, as the fashion for little boys then was, came up so high, I could, with a slight effort, lick the white bone button that came through my brace. After one glance of envy at Fred as he went out happy in the freedom of old clothes, I resigned myself to making a watch-chain of the cherry-stones I had been hoarding and grinding thin for several weeks ; and then Mary joined me, and sat in a rocking-chair, and hemmed a muslin blind for the gentleman boarder's window.

The great clock in the Pavilion tower suddenly sounded on the hot drowsy air.

"Run, Harry," said Mary, "and see if Mother and Sukie are coming, and if you can carry anything for them : it is three already."

I clambered off my chair, and ran through the office, and met Mother and Sukie with full baskets coming up the steps. My Mother looked hot, and a little

Our Gentleman Boarder

flustered, and her bonnet was the least awry, but her hands were too full to right it.

"Lord, child, what a day!" she gasped, and went by me into the parlour. "Come in, Sukie," she said, "and bring the fruit for Miss Mary to see."

Sukie, looking equally hot and a little subdued, obeyed, and I, with eyes on a basket of cherries, followed them in.

"Why, Mother, how hot and tired you are!" said Mary, relieving her of her burden, and going about to remove her shawl.

My Mother waved her off feebly and sank into a chair. "Tired?" she said. "Tired? I should think I was, and yet not a step further than round the New Market!"

"And quite far enough too," said Sukie, wiping her brow and cheeks with her handkerchief.

"There now!" cried my Mother, almost hysterically; and she undid her bonnet ribbons to laugh the easier, and flung them back over her shoulders. "To hear her! O Sukie!" and then she fell to laughing in the way one may in hot weather, when in such limp and enfeebled condition one is at the mercy of the smallest comicality.

Our Gentleman Boarder

Mary, full of her business and anxious that Sukie should get about hers, asked a little quickly where lay the joke, and went to her hemming with great energy.

Sukie looked the least defiantly at my Mother, and said, " You may laugh, Mrs. Hyde, but, for all that, I believe it's a kind of tempting of Providence."

" She means," said my Mother, " she means—O Mary, only just round the Market," and off she went again, so that I caught the infection and rolled on the carpet with laughing.

" Does Mother mean," said Mary, beginning to smile herself, and, with an eye to the spotlessness of my breeks, raising me from the floor, " that you were afraid to go round the Market?"

" She *do*," said Sukie, " and quite right too. So I was; and so I am. What with the crossing of the roads, which alone is only fit for horses and carts, and then in the market with folk on this side of you, and folk on that, and folk a-foolin' all round, why, why it's enough to make a sober woman feel like t'other kind !"

" Haven't you ever been into the New Market before?" chimed in I, all a-grin, and knowing quite well that she never went elsewhere than to her father. " Why,

Our Gentleman Boarder

Sukie, I know my way all over Brighton alone, and *I'm* not afraid."

" Brats is different," she snapped, turning very red ; and then Mary broke into laughter.

" Poor old Sukie," she said kindly, but with twinkling eyes, " however came it to pass that you got home safe after all ? "

" Why she just clung to my shawl the whole way," whimpered my Mother behind her handkerchief.

" Thank God I did," said Sukie, feeling it were better to brave the whole thing out. " Yes," she added, defiantly, " I don't care who knows. I held as fast as I could, and I shut my eyes as fast as they'd go crossing that road, and then in that hustle-bustle I kept as close as close, for I thought every moment may be I'd be lost."

" But surely you could have asked your way if you had—not that that is a possibility either, so few yards from our door," said Mary, bent now on drawing her out and enjoying the fun as far as kindliness would allow. " Surely you could have asked your way of some one ! "

Sukie left off mopping her face and looked knowing. " Ah, but they tells you such lies," she said. " They tells you such

Our Gentleman Boarder

lies. No, I tell ye, Miss Mary," she went on, quite earnestly, "I don't think I could go through with it again to-day, not if it was to fetch marketing for all the gentlemen boarders in the world."

"Well, well," said Mary, "go along and prepare those lettuces; but I wish you could get more accustomed to the streets, Sukie, dear; it would be better for your health and comfort."

To which Sukie, gathering up her baskets and bags preparatory to departing, murmured, "O, if it's for health and comfort, give me four good walls, say I;" and really, considering that she never had any complaint from one year's end to another, her remark was not without weight.

Then Mary and Mother began picking over the cherries for tea, and Mother gave me four for myself, joined two and two by their stalks, which I hung over my ears by way of decoration. They discussed the expected guest until I burned with curiosity to see him.

"Old Mr. Trevanion tells your Father that the young gentleman is very melancholy at times," said Mother, thoughtfully.

I plucked Mary's sleeve. "What's melancholy?" I asked under my breath.

"Low spirited," she replied, "like you

Our Gentleman Boarder

are when you have sat up too late the night before : like you are when you know mother is going to give you a dose of senna.—A little sea air, and sea bathing, and some talk with Father will soon cure him of that," she added, "unless indeed he is an unusually poor kind of creature."

"Little pitchers!" said my Mother, looking at her meaningly and following up the remark with a cough. "Now Harry, mind," Mother continued, turning to me, "when the coach comes in you and Fred are not to go hanging about, and staring at the gentleman, as you do sometimes. It's not nice manners, especially when he's going to live with us afterwards."

I was a little disappointed at this, having purposed meeting the coach in the square, so as to have a good look at the low spirited gentleman; for I was filled with a lively recollection of my own condition when a certain little yellow mug brimming with senna tea awaited my agonised gulps; and I expected to find him suffused in tears and partly hidden by his handkerchief.

In a little space came Sukie, and Mother and Mary must shift their work, for she was going to spread the table with a clean white cloth. Then was it time for Mary to take her keys and release from the old

Our Gentleman Boarder

corner-cupboard the little household gods. I was quite awe-stricken when I found they were all to come out into use, for it was not even Sunday or Christmas. There were six silver teaspoons and sugar-nippers, given to Mary on her christening day by an old passenger of my Father's, a china teapot, with two handles twisted prettily together, a big muffineer, and a dish that had been given my father by a poor French gentleman whom he had helped in some fashion or other, a beautiful thing with festoons of tiny roses upon it, and little true love-knots in blue, and, lastly, the cups and saucers that we only used on Sundays, these last being the darling treasure of my Mother, for they had been given her as the best needlewoman in the village, on the occasion of her marriage, by the great lady of the place. I remember all those little treasures of ours, not only because they were so few, but rather by reason of their several pleasant histories. John Müller, Esther's sweetheart, had brought her a gay posy, all of pinks and mignonette and sweet william, that morning from his mother's garden, and when Mary placed these in the centre of the table it really looked as dainty as you please.

Our Gentleman Boarder

"Making mighty fine fuss all for a stranger," said Sukie, glancing nevertheless with some pride at the table.

"Now, Susan," said my Mother, with a

hint of warning in her tone, "you mustn't say that sort of thing when the gentleman is here; remember, he is accustomed to everything elegant and convenient in his own home, and he will pay for the best here."

Our Gentleman Boarder

"Ah, well, there's one good thing," continued Sukie, rubbing up the tea-caddy with her apron, "stranger he is, but he's not one of them nasty French critturs."

Mary told her a little stiffly that if she could not speak in civil fashion of our friends she need make no mention of them. The little packet from Dieppe not infrequently brought us a visitor at that period, for my brother William had been in France, and had formed several friendships there. Sukie had a great dislike of all foreigners, and, being still a little ruffled from her marketing terrors, was glad of an opportunity for airing her silly prejudice,

"I don't know if it's rude or not," she said, obstinately, "but true it *is*; any one as don't squint could see at a glance that they ain't like us; they look quite different; they ain't natural, to my mind. And, then, their silly ways! I've no patience with them to hear them jabberin' their nonsense at you and you jabberin' it all back again—it do rile me!"

"It's not nonsense at all, Susan," broke in my mother, "it's their language, and Miss Mary speaks it beautifully—every one tells me so."

"Language, indeed!" she chirped, in an amused fashion. "Why can't they speak

Our Gentleman Boarder

good plain English, like other folks? It's good enough for me; and they could if they liked; it's only their nasty deceit."

The sound of the guard's bugle, at no great distance, interrupted the discussion and threw my Mother into a great fluster.

"There, run, Harry, and see your Father —no, don't, child; you're sure to stare too much. There, I've never taken off my bonnet, after all!" and she jumped up and gathered up her shawl and other belongings preparatory to flight.

"Everything is ready," said Mary; "I will receive the gentleman, if you like, and Harry shall show him his room."

And then the place became all astir, and, spying through the door into the office, I saw the coach drawing up. Sprightly and Varney and the other ostlers ran out of the yard, the guard held the ladder and received the tips of the passengers with nods and grins and "Thank'ee, sir," and then there was a great chatter, with kissing and laughing; for people had been gathering round the office for some minutes past, awaiting the coming in of friends on the coach. Seeing my Father get down from the box, I left my spy-chink and ran into the passage, there to encounter Sprightly carrying a portmanteau upstairs.

Our Gentleman Boarder

"Spright, Spright!" I called, in a loud whisper. "Is he melancholy?" and I cut a caper.

"My eye, ain't 'e, tho'!" said Sprightly, and passed out of sight with an outrageous wink, without comprehending my question in the least.

"This, sir," I heard my Father's voice saying, "is my daughter Mary; our housekeeper, and I hope she'll make you comfortable here."

I listened painfully outside the door to catch the reply of the low-spirited gentleman.

"It is very good of you all to receive a stranger into your midst, Miss Hyde," I heard a pleasant voice say, and then I ventured to enter and look at the victim of melancholia.

"I hope, sir," said Mary, with a curtsey, and small boy as I was, I felt that Mary had very pretty manners, "that you will find your visit a pleasant one, and that you will enjoy our fine Brighton air. This is our little brother Harry," she said, as she noticed me, and she bade me show Mr. Trevanion to his own room. Shy as I was, I had made friends with this pleasant gentleman before we reached his door.

Even in the course of that first evening

Our Gentleman Boarder

our gentleman boarder, who chose to spend it with us rather than in his own sitting-room, won his way into all our hearts. He was full of interesting talk, charmingly spiced with humour, and was very gentle

in manner. As to the melancholy disposition, we saw no trace of it, unless it were in the face, which was extremely refined and something worn, considering his twenty-three years, and a little look of Lord Byron, said Esther, about the cut of his clothes.

He endeared himself to us all in a very

Our Gentleman Boarder

short space. My Father he treated always with respect, and even affection, and won my Mother's heart by his kindly attentions and his readiness to help with her wool-winding ; he threaded her needles too, and told her he had long done that for his mother, who was an invalid, and considered he could now thread a needle with any woman in England ! With Esther, who was as merry as a June grasshopper in those days, he had many a bantering bout, and he taught us boys several pretty conjuring tricks, and constituted himself umpire in our pillow-fights.

But with Mary he was a far more serious creature. To her he brought the treasures of his book-shelf, lending them, or reading them with her if she could but spare the time. And he took great pleasure in listening to her comments and criticism ; for Mary was gifted with a clear, quick mind, and through never having read any but classic, if rather antiquated authors, had unconsciously developed a fine literary taste ; and then too whatever she loved and believed in the books she read, she made her own, in a lasting intimate fashion, hard to find among girls in this generation of cheap periodicals and yellow-back novels.

Many years before, a little girl, carrying a

Our Gentleman Boarder

baby in her arms, accosted a clergyman of our town as he was leaving the church after morning service, and looking up at him with glowing face, asked him in a voice trembling betwixt shyness and expectation, if he would be so very kind as to lend her a book to read. She wanted very much to read, she said, and indeed could find time to do so when she had put the children to bed of a night; but they had no books at home save the Bible and Prayer Book, and Pilgrim's Progress, all of which, she said naïvely, she knew quite well; and he might rest assured his book would be taken good care of, because her father was Mr. Hyde the coachmaster.

The heart of the gentle old student was greatly touched, and before long the bright-eyed, hardworking child, with her hunger and thirst after learning, was admitted to his library, and enjoyed the run of it in such spare time as she had until his death, when he left her as a parting gift a charming handful of old poets and dramatists.

Now I am quite prepared for my readers, when they find the simple narrative blooming into a love tale, to cry out upon me for a precocious imp, that could so comprehend and remember the deeds and words of his elders in such a matter ; or to accuse me

Our Gentleman Boarder

of filling up a vague outline of truth with details of my own imagining. Therefore I will at once acknowledge that for much in what I tell I am indebted to my Mother, who, when I grew old enough, confided to me more than once the whole sad little story of Mary's love. And on the other hand I must confess to a certain precocity of sympathy in my childhood, which caught at and stored up in a very tender heart many things which I could not wholly comprehend. Words and looks, where my heart was stirred, were imprinted upon my memory, even while the facts that lay behind them were widely out of range of my immature understanding.

It soon became a usual occurrence for Mary and Mr. Trevanion to read together for a while before tea. My Mother was a little discomfited by this, and hunted up many an unnecessary task which should keep Mary occupied at that time; but love would find out the way in this case as in all others. Mr. Trevanion took great delight in the French language, and sang charming songs in that tongue to his guitar in the evenings: very helpless and alarmed my Mother felt one time, when Esther, the only one of us beside Mary who knew what the words were about, broke out into

Our Gentleman Boarder

a ripple of laughter, while Mary bent her head lower over her work, and stitched away with more than her usual energy.

Very few months had passed since the coach had brought the disturber of the peace into our midst, when Mr. Trevanion told my parents that he loved Mary, and asked permission to make her his wife. He spoke in a very impassioned and beautiful manner, which won my Mother at once. My Father was amazed beyond telling : he had neither seen nor suspected the little love story that had been unfolding itself, chapter by chapter, before his eyes from the very day upon which he had introduced his passenger to Mary in the little parlour.

"Why, you dear old silly," said my Mother, "haven't I told you till I was tired that I knew this would happen ? *I* saw it long ago, I felt *sure* of it."

"But, my tender soul," said my Father, still bewildered, "I didn't believe you, did I ? Women are always feeling sure about something, bless them!"

He soon came out of his bewilderment into a state of glee. He went about the house, rubbing his hands, and smiling, and saying, "God bless them!" whenever he thought of it, and was as happy as a child,

Our Gentleman Boarder

for he was very much attached to the young fellow; and as for Mary, she was a queen of girls to him, and deserved all the happiness in the world. Like a child, too, he ignored all the difficulties of the situation, the wide difference in social position, and Mary's lack of money, and said simply, when Mother thrummed restlessly on this string of poverty, "But they'll never be poor, will they? His father's a very rich old gentleman, and there's enough for them all, I should say, for all she can't bring any money bags to the marriage;" for which my mother laughed at him soundly.

"I should have thought you might have seen by this time," she said, shaking her head shrewdly, "that it's money bags that marry money bags; it's only your labourer with his nine shillings a week that can afford to marry a penniless maid."

The difficulty of the difference of social position he grasped somewhat more easily.

"I see, I see," he said, slowly; "that does look like an awkward bit of road, because you see Mary is not that kind of girl that wouldn't like us to come and see her now and again; nor she isn't one to be content unless she could ask us into the best parlour, is she?"

My Mother was really in painful per-

Our Gentleman Boarder

plexity; she knew full well that the young man's parents would be highly incensed at their son's behaviour and would, as a matter of course, accuse my Mother of connivance, when in very truth the good soul had done her utmost to keep the young people apart. On the other hand, she was satisfied in her own mind that it was a very true love that had grown between them, and she knew well the unusual worth of her daughter. To that bright mind and upright character, almost austere in its strength, she had looked for guidance and help from Mary's very childhood, wondering sometimes at her own dependence and with a secret reverence. She knew that Mary well deserved all the happiness possible in such a union and her motherly heart desired it for her child. But she had enough of worldly wisdom to know that the obstacles were well-nigh impassable, and that there are people in this world whom no charm of mind or person will reconcile to a homeliness of parentage. She had a very earnest talk with Mary when she came to tell her that Mr. Trevanion was only waiting her consent to the engagement to write and ask his parents for theirs. She told her that they should not allow themselves to hope that Mr. Trevanion's family would receive

Our Gentleman Boarder

the news otherwise than with anger and contempt. She implored Mary not to let her present happiness run away with her reason, but to brace herself for a harsh rebuff.

"I have thought of it continually, Mother," Mary said, "and I have told Mr. Trevanion I could not possibly become engaged to him, if after all right argument they still oppose it. I hope they will give me a fair chance," she went on earnestly, "that they will see me before they give their final answer. Mr. Trevanion says his father is especially tender-hearted and would soon like me well enough."

I think Mother must have looked at her with some pride. Mary was only twenty, as fresh as a flower, and with a certain dignity of presence which had naught to do with size, for she was slender and none too tall. She had beautiful hair and Saxon blue eyes, very grave and intent, when the gleam of passing fun was out of them.

"Yes, dear, I hope they'll see you, I'm sure," said the Mother. She was never very demonstrative with Mary, nor Mary with her, but she put up her hands as she spoke to stroke the girl's soft sunny hair, a little shyly, for Mary usually showed her-

Our Gentleman Boarder

self embarrassed under caresses. "But even then there'll be difficulties; there's little doubt they will have thought of someone else for him, a very different kind of person, rich, and a lady."

"I am a lady, Mother dear," said Mary, simply; and indeed it was an undeniable truth.

"But then," added my Mother, smiling and flushing a little pathetically, "there's us, dear. Wouldn't it be a little uncomfortable for you to have people like that belonging to you?"

"Mother!" said Mary, reproachfully: they understood each other. "You see, dear," she went on, "I shall never be the grand person you imagine, nor live the grand life you think. I told him I could not marry a man who would ask me to do so. He does not wish it, he tells me; it was all the frivolity of the great world that made him so melancholy, and that he has left it for ever. He says he felt just like a boy going home for the holidays when our coach brought him to Brighton. We should lead a quiet life in the country, and study, and Arthur says I am to go on with the translation of my old French poets, and we shall try to live a kindly simple life with plenty of books and a sweet old

Our Gentleman Boarder

garden, and visits from all of you from time to time."

Mother looked at Mary; she was radiant in the thought of the life she described; then Mother sighed.

Arthur Trevanion wrote his letter, which he read to my parents before sending away. My Father was delighted with it, and said it was beautiful and touching. The writer addressed his parents most dutifully and affectionately and asked when he might bring Mary to see them—that to see her was to love her, &c., all of which, as my Father naïvely said as he wiped his eyes, was "as pretty as a play."

He never received any direct acknowledgement of his news : there came first a silly little letter from his mother, who was an invalid, saying, *à propos* of nothing at all, that she felt every day of her life more convinced that any grief or shock would kill her; and a long letter from his uncle, a bishop, who was also his godfather, which, after a long preamble expressing his joy in his dear nephew's fully recovered health, trailed off into the necessity of travel as a completing of education, and so, in a curiously irrelevant fashion, to the glorious privilege of the Christian of sacrificing all personal desires and ambitions to the sacred

Our Gentleman Boarder

claims of duty, "which, being interpreted," said Mr. Trevanion, bitterly, "means the world and the devil, with just so much of the flesh thrown in, as a bishop must wink at in Society."

Shortly after the receipt of these came a messenger in hot haste from London, bearing a letter bidding Mr. Trevanion return home at once, and thence sail for India as quickly as possible, as bad news had been received of the Indian branch of the great banking house, and the presence of a member of the family was vitally necessary at this critical time.

He received the summons, following as it did the foolish and insulting letters, with a passionate outburst of anger ; a word from Mary would have induced him to break there and then with his family, but Mary, with her quiet pride and her strong sense of duty towards parents, had no such word for him.

For hours they had been threshing out all the possibilities of the situation, and still to her there appeared no near prospect of a rightfully happy issue.

"You must go," she said. "Perhaps we shall meet again some day."

"Some day!" he cried, bitterly. "How coldly you can say it. I shall go out to

Our Gentleman Boarder

India and put things straight and come back as quickly as I can and claim you in spite of every one; and if by any unhappy chance I have to live out there, you will come with me, will you not, Mary?"

"I fear that does not end our difficulties," said Mary, with a little smile, but her bright eyes had no smile in them. "I have told you I could not live far away from my parents. That is quite certain, you see."

"But, Mary," he said, rather impatiently, "surely Esther can look after them!"

"Esther? She would, I know, but she is going to be married before very long; besides, she is not hearty and strong like I am—indeed, I sometimes fear she is very, very delicate. "Oh," she added, desperately, while the tears welled up in her eyes, "you *must* see how they need me at times. You must see it—every one who lives here must see it. I hope you will understand it—will try to understand how things are with me."

The tone of Mary's voice startled me out of my "Robinson Crusoe;" I knew she was dreadfully unhappy, and that made me feel very dismal. I remember many things that she said, though I cannot truly give his replies. I was only thinking of her.

"I was going on day by day contented

Our Gentleman Boarder

and proud in their love and their dependence, and I think I could have gone on so for ever, had you not come here or anywhere else across my road. You have done away with all that now; you have made me want my life for myself and—and for you. I am not cold; I have been as happy in the thought of being your wife as any woman ever could be, and now that you are going right away, and so many things forbid our marriage, I want that happiness as dearly as any woman that ever lived; but I know what is right all the while. I want you not to misunderstand me," she said, looking up into his eyes in a sad, passionate kind of way that made me feel ashamed of being there. " Life is hard to bear as it is."

I heard Mary say that; I was the only other soul in the room, and I think they were too wretched to mind me; if they thought of me at all, they very likely considered me too small and too much engrossed in my picture-book to heed or understand their words. Nevertheless, I went to bed very downhearted, and not a little perplexed that night. As far as I know, that was the first and last occasion on which my sister Mary confessed to any hardship or burden in her devoted life.

Our Gentleman Boarder

Mr. Trevanion, keeping a desperate grip on hope, told my Father and Mother that he was going back to his parents to try what personal pleading could effect in bringing them to see the matter in a kindlier light.

"My Father is very tender-hearted, in reality," he said, eagerly, seeing my Mother shake her head; "I am sure I can win him over, and, indeed, it is quite possible he will let me go out there, do what I can to put things right, and then return to England for good."

The evening before his departure was a sad time, though my Father did his best to make it cheerful; he bade Mother prepare as pretty a supper as possible, and he himself fetched up a choice bottle of wine, one of half a dozen sent him by an old passenger many a Christmas back.

"There's just two bottles, and it is prime stuff, I can tell you!" he said, jollily, "and we'll drink one now, just as a 'God speed' to you on your voyage, sir, and the other we'll leave till you come back. Ah, Mother, you *will* have to make us a fine supper the day Mr. Trevanion comes home again and we drink the other bottle, eh?"

We boys were allowed to sit up late as it was the last evening, but we did not enjoy it, although Father sang "Giles

Our Gentleman Boarder

Scroggins," which he only did at Christmas, as a rule. But if to us the evening proved disappointingly dull and sleepy, I know now that for the others it was a trial time indeed, oppressive with its demand for assumed confidence and jollity, in every lull of which the ever present though unacknowledged trouble leapt up and took one by the throat. My interest in the proceedings revived a little when Esther, anxious to end one such ominous pause, broke into guessing at the various treasures and curiosities Mr. Trevanion would bring home with him in a twelvemonth's time. Fred asked for a monkey, and I bargained for a parrot and a baby tiger ; but even that pleasure was fleeting, for on turning to my Mother with "What'll you choose, mother ? It's your turn now!" I found she was quietly crying to herself over her knitting; which put me quite out of countenance.

Next morning, and a cheerless drizzling day it was, Mr. Trevanion bade us all good-bye. He was very pale, and looked far more like the "melancholy gentleman" than he had done when he arrived that hot summer afternoon. I noted with some satisfaction that Mary and he and myself were the only people who did not cry;

Our Gentleman Boarder

Fred was in school or there had of a certainty been a fourth pair of dry eyes. When last of all he came to Mary and took her hand, and strove to say I know not what, she smiled up at him bravely, and then they kissed one another very earnestly and frankly before us all, the which, with a girl as good and as proud as our Mary, was a pledge and acceptance of life-long faith. Then he turned and went out quickly, and a minute later he was waving his hat to us as the coach rattled away through the mist, leaving us behind in an empty unkind day.

Whether that last bottle of wine was ever opened I do not know; but it certainly was not brought out on the occasion for which my Father so long reserved it, for Mr. Trevanion never returned. Mary wrote two several times to him, and although we heard of his safety and well-doing, she received no reply, so she wrote no more and spoke of him no more. Nor did we ever hear any explanation of this conduct, extraordinary in one, who, though perhaps a little weak and easily led, was undeniably a gentleman, and a tender-hearted one too. I can only think he was worked upon or bound to a vow under threat of some heartrending alternative,

Our Gentleman Boarder

probably the death of his mother, whom he loved so dearly, and whose delicate wire-pulling could sway the sensitive nature which paternal wrath might strive in vain to move. Or else the great world from which he had so long exiled himself proved too immediately bewitching in the welcome it accorded this charming and popular prodigal. However it be, God help all poor souls, say I, that have pathetic, albeit worldly invalids for mothers, and bishops for godfathers, backed as these will surely be by the approval of society; for, failing the Divine succour, they are lost for a certainty to all true and wholesome life!

What suffering Mary endured we knew not, for we never saw her in tears after his departure, but she was restlessly anxious for work, always work, and grew a little irritable now and again if any one spoke to her in a too compassionate tone. One Sunday afternoon, Esther, all aglow and happy from a walk with her sweetheart came singing into the parlour where Mary and I were sitting. Recognising the book Mary was reading, a little volume of French poetry from which Mr. Trevanion had often read aloud to her, her look changed as if she were stricken with pity and a kind of shame at her own gladness. She went

Our Gentleman Boarder

up to her sister and put her arms about her and laid her pretty head upon her shoulder.

"Dear, dear Mary," she said, tearfully.

Mary put her away and closed the book. "Don't, dear," she said quite gently, and left the room.

She loved Arthur Trevanion whole heartedly. He was the first man beside her father and brother she had ever deemed it possible to love, the first man she had ever met on her own level of thought and feeling. His love had glorified every hour of her work-a-day present, and had shown her the future as a new created world, where all her long-pent aspirations might dare to try their wings, and all her dreams find their most sacred fulfilment. But since he did not need her, since her love was so little to him what his love was to her, her pride rose irresistibly and cut her off from all possible discussion of him, or his motives and reasons. She wanted the little world she lived in to think that for her he no longer existed, that he had gone utterly out of her heart and thought, and she bore herself as if this were indeed the truth, however she may have clung to him in secret hope and passionate prayer. From that time she treated all idea of marriage for herself as a curious

Our Gentleman Boarder

and unpleasing impossibility, though she was full of sympathy with other folks' love-troubles. Before her hair went grey, several very worthy fellows went away with the heartache from her quiet and absolute refusal.

As for Mr. Trevanion, we heard in about a twelvemonth's time he was getting on well in India, having developed an unexpected business capacity: and a little later still that he was living like a veritable nabob in Calcutta, where he had married a young lady who had chanced to make the outward voyage with himself, a very charming girl they said, and the heiress of a Calcutta millionaire whose name is blazoned throughout the earth on the labels of unnumbered jars of chutnee and other pickles.

A DAY OF PUNISHMENT

THE day began badly; I got out of bed with my wrong leg foremost, and shortly afterwards knocked my funny-bone against the washstand; I dawdled over my dressing, and on entering the kitchen was severely taken to task by Mary for my lie-a-bed ways, and bidden be quick and make up for lost time: but her chiding was all to no purpose, for I was possessed by the very devil of deliberateness that morning. I leisurely seated myself at the table, and lavishly buttered the bread I ate with my slice of cold ham, regardless of Mary's housewifely feelings: then I sipped the milk and water in my mug and gave an audible shudder.

"Well, what's the matter now?" said Mary, bustling about the kitchen with all the offensive activity of an early riser.

A Day of Punishment

"There's not enough sugar," I grumbled.

"'Tis as much as you'll get, my dear," she said, in a mild and exasperating tone, not forgetful of that undue spread of butter. Thereupon I leaned back in my chair with my hands in my pockets, and drubbed my shoes against the rail.

"Why, you've not eaten your ham yet!' she exclaimed, with assumed surprise, which grown people imagine will turn the tide of childish ill-humour."

"Don't like it," I said.

"Fiddlesticks!" she replied, with a mingle of cheeriness and sharpness in her tone that grated on my nerves, and humming to herself she went about her work in the outhouse. She returned in the course of a few minutes with a pile of clean willow-pattern plates, and remarked, as she arranged them on the dresser, "If you are not going to eat any more you had better be off to school, for it is very late already." I might have gone of my own accord if she had not said that, but that just gave the cue to my devil. With the utmost *sangfroid* I drew a tee-to-tum from my pocket and began to spin it on the bread trencher.

Before I had guessed her intention

A Day of Punishment

Mary took my chair by the back and swung me away from the table.

"Don't be a little fool, Harry," she said, quietly.

I leapt from my chair, seized my plate, and shoved it across the table so hard that it fell and broke on the floor. "I don't want your ugly old breakfast," I cried, and flung out of the room, to hear my sister say with a little quaver of anger in her voice, "All right, Master Harry, your Father shall hear of this to-night when he comes home;" and then, slightly raising her voice as I retreated, "No Lewes Fair for *you* next week, young gentleman!"

I ran up to my room to fetch my satchel, and when I came down again I heard Mary recounting the history of my ill-deeds to Mother, and I heard Mother cry out on me for my wanton behaviour to her china; and then Sukie must needs air her opinion and declare that, for her part, she thought I had been like a little bear with a sore head this many days, and that a good dose of senna would not be amiss; and they all agreed that a stop should be put to it.

Feeling it beneath my dignity to listen to such idle talk, I left the house, nor did I forget to slam the door behind me, in the

A Day of Punishment

doing of which I relieved myself of a particle of my superabundant naughtiness. A few yards on ahead of me I spied a schoolfellow, a weak-eyed boy who was always late, and had a mother who beat him sometimes, when she was not sober. I came up quietly behind him and, whisking his cap into the middle of the road by way of greeting, suggested that we should go school-wards by way of the beach (which was as who should say, standing at the north end of Portland Place, " Let us go to Tottenham Court Road by way of Oxford Street ") : this he agreed to with enthusiasm, and we jogged along merrily enough. We had a match in the throwing of ducks and drakes, and my last vestige of ill-humour cleared off when I realised that my prowess in this art was greater than Jack's. There is nothing in the world so soothing to one's temper as the tickling of one's vanity : 'tis a fine counter-irritant.

We certainly took our time and eventually arrived at Mr. Blocker's door in the best of tempers and on three legs, having tied our two neighbouring limbs together with my handkerchief ; and as we were freeing ourselves with a monstrous giggling in the porch, Jack was so smitten

A Day of Punishment

with the beauty of my handkerchief, with its gaily printed pictures and verses of Dame Hubbard and her dog, that I gave it to him there and then.

We entered the schoolroom, I with a little swagger to cover my own uneasiness in my tardy appearance, and Jack all agrin with pleasure in having at last a comrade to share his daily rebuke. But I soon noticed with some dismay that Mr. Blocker was looking at me over the tops of his spectacles with a severity quite disproportionate to my slight offence.

" Master Hyde," he said, awfully, " stand up." Master Hyde stood up and tried to look as if he rather liked the situation.

"What's this I hear of you, sir ? " he said in a certain voice which always betokened corporal punishment. " I have here a letter from your worthy Mother telling me that your conduct this morning has been in the highest degree disgraceful, indeed, utterly unwarrantable in a lad of your years and careful Christian training ; and she has desired me to inflict some severe punishment on you.

The memory of my encounter with Mary came upon me like a sudden cloud across the sun ; I had quite forgotten it in my recovered good humour.

A Day of Punishment

" So they have told of me, have they ? " I thought ; "and just to disgrace me before all the boys." My heart beat thick with anger and shame, and I think all the blood in my body rushed up into my hot little face.

" Master Hyde, come here."

I wriggled myself out between the long desk and the purposely thrust out knees of the grinning boys and went up and stood before the master.

Mr. Blocker always made a great point of cross-examining his victims before punishing them. In extracting the whole dreary story, down to its most inconsiderable detail, from the lips of the small and quaking wretch before him, I think he believed he was satisfying all reasonable demands of justice ; but to us boys the advantage of this painful process was not apparent, for whether we pleaded " guilty " or " not guilty," we were invariably chastised.

" Now, sir," said Mr. Blocker, settling himself comfortably in his chair, as was his custom when about to listen to a recitation, " have the kindness to tell me what it was that you said or did, and in what precise manner you offended."

I looked him full in the eyes, and closed

A Day of Punishment

my lips more significantly than civilly. "All right, old fellow," I thought; "if you don't know *I'm* not going to tell you."

Mr. Blocker drew his turnip watch from his fob and laid it, with a little clatter of its seal and charms, on the desk before him. "I give you two minutes," he said.

There was an absolute silence; the boys even refrained from giggling, so keen were they to lose no breath or syllable of the torture. Mr. Blocker looked at his watch, then at me, and his face grew ominously red; he was a very passionate old man, and yet, in some ways, a good sort of fellow.

"If you obstinately insist in holding your tongue, Master Hyde, I shall proceed to punish you without further parley." He felt about in his desk for something, and found it—a little strap with a buckle at one end.

"Hold out your hand, sir." I held it out as steady as I could, for I was mad lest the boys should take the tremble of anger for that of fear. And, indeed, I was angry; I was like to have choked with the beating of my fierce little heart. That my people should have told tales about me, instead of punishing me themselves, that they should have gone about to disgrace me without

A Day of Punishment

fair warning! It was intolerable; they had, according to my notions of honour at that time, sneaked and taken a mean advantage. A dozen times he brought the buckle end of the strap down on my brown paw, and twice the buckle curled round and cut my knuckles; but I felt I would die rather than cry. That exasperated him, I think; he pushed his spectacles on to the top of his head and asked me, with the peculiar glare of a short-sighted person, whether I had had enough or no. I made no reply, and disdained to withdraw my hand.

"Have you had enough, sir?" he thundered.

I longed to say no, but I could not utter a sound. He again turned to his desk and brought thence a long conical-shaped cap made of paper; it was ever the climax of torture for sensitive children in those days, and, true to its form, invariably succeeded in extinguishing the last flicker of self-respect and hope in the insulted little being that wore it. This he placed on my head, in a way that thrust my ears unnaturally outwards, then he looked at me for a second or so, wiped his forehead, and said, "Get on the stool." Now, the stool was one of repentance, and being long in the legs, was yet stood upon an inverted

A Day of Punishment

packing-case; and it had neither back nor foot-rail.

"Now, you others," cried Mr. Blocker, when, speechless with rage and misery, I

A Day of Punishment

had hoisted myself on to the stool, "take notice that Master Hyde is not to be spoken to or played with for the rest of the day."

A slight buzz of whispering and a half-suppressed cackle of laughter followed this announcement, and then the lads betook themselves to their tasks with more zest than usual, for the incident and the sight of my ludicrous position introduced a new interest into the dull school hours.

For a little while I sat looking straight down my nose, frightfully conscious of the grins and grimaces of my young friends, but knowing before long that their interest had somewhat subsided, I ventured to glance at the various slates and heads beneath me.

What a revelation was there! I saw the schoolmaster drowsing between the paragraphs of the *Brighton Herald* while he kept the boys to work out a sum he had set them; I saw the weak-eyed boy, my companion of that morning, decorating the form beside him with his own initials writ large in adhesive gelatine lozenges; I saw Fred Tapps, the acknowledged wag of the school, drawing on his slate his famous caricature of Mr. Blocker, which, when he caught my eye, he promptly spat upon,

A Day of Punishment

rubbing it out with the sleeve of his jacket, while he thrust out his tongue at me; and then I saw a peppermint bull's-eye bartered for permission to copy the working of the sum figure for figure. I saw all this and more, and the thought came into my head that my bird's-eye view must be very similar to that which Providence has of this naughty world, myself included.

"Please sir," suddenly shrilled the master's son, and he made me jump, for I was following up the train of thought; he was a shifty, feeble-minded boy who never looked you in the face, for all he was so keen to detect a mote in your eye—"Please sir, here's Master Giles catching our flies," he said.

Mr. Blocker looked a little foolish and none too pleased, and addressing himself apparently to the furthest form of all, whereas his son sat immediately beneath his father's desk, said sharply, "No talking in class if you please," and then sought sanctuary from the score of grinning faces behind the leaves of his *Herald*.

I was too miserable to feel much interest in any of the doings and soon gave up noticing them, fixing my eyes sometimes on the old brown Mercator's Projection hanging on the opposite wall, or tracing

A Day of Punishment

caricature resemblances to all my friends and relations in the lines of the cracked plaster; this last affording me some little grim pleasure.

Suddenly I caught the eye of Master Blocker, and in sheer bravado I grinned at him. Up went his hand to hail his father's attention, "Please sir, Master Hyde's a larfin," piped the mean imp, and roused the master, who, what with irritation at the second interruption of his morning's reading, and an overwhelming certainty that I must have been laughing at *him*, flew into a very fine rage, dragged me down from the stool and shook me till I could hardly see. "I'll mend your manners for you, you young cub," he said; and then followed such a thrashing as I hope no child may ever again endure; beginning with flash upon flash of stinging pain, growing by repetition to a steady flame of agony; while every cut that he gave me lashed the man himself into a blinder fury, and made the room for me spin round and round like a tee-to-tum, until utterly unable to stand I curled up and fell at his feet. Even then, swish, swish came the cane over my arms and neck until his own arm must have fairly ached. Bending over me with the palsy of rage in his every limb and a breathless

A Day of Punishment

tremor in his voice, he said, "Get up, get up with you at once, and don't let me have any more of your d——d shamming."

I crawled on to my hands and knees and somehow, but I never knew how, I scrambled on to the stool again, happily not for long, or I should probably have fainted and fallen.

Almost immediately after this, school broke up and I was bidden descend, and told that lunch would be sent to me in the schoolroom, as my mother would not suffer me to return home for dinner. I spent that dinner-hour staring at the hunk of bread and cheese they sent me and brooding desperately over my wrongs; I was aching in every atom of my body and nearly insane with rebellion. A maid-servant came to fetch my plate away, and I was hot and cold with terror lest she should speak kindly to me; but she went her way without speaking, merely observing to some one outside the door, "He ain't took a single bite!"

Knowing that the boys returned at two I determined to remount the stool before that time, and when they came trooping in, they found me again perched, Providence-like, over their heads. Mr. Blocker was a little surprised at this, and for a moment

A Day of Punishment

appeared at a loss. He had had an excellent dinner, and the rage of the passionate man had subsided into the purely professional severity of the schoolmaster.

"Who told you to get up there again?" he said. "I desire that another time you will await my orders before you do anything of the kind. Come down at once!"

I thought at the time, he said this that I might make my ludicrous and difficult descent before the boys, and I hated him accordingly; but I know now that it was from motives of humanity, for I must have looked very pale, I fancy. He set me a copy: "Honour thy Father and thy Mother," he said, reading the words aloud in a slow and meaning manner, and bade me take and write it at a desk standing apart from all the others. It quite failed in making the desired impression. I felt little fear of curtailing the length of my days in the land by my conduct of that morning, for Mary was only a sister; and as I took the book from his hand I was moved with secret scorn to think how wide of the mark he was.

Many years later I held in my hands for half an hour a florid but beautiful fifteenth-century missal, and as I looked I realised that in this way of cunning fantastical line

A Day of Punishment

and gorgeous pigment, the artist-monk had given rein to the pent passions and power of his nature ; and I laughed, for at that very moment there leapt within me the memory of myself as a small imp writing that copy, letting out my mute embittered soul in deep-dug curves and spider-fine up-strokes, and curl within curl of the capital letters, and with as many a touch of caricature as I dared in that demon-possessed mood run to.

To a child whose whole person aches with recent chastisement, whose heart is unutterably full, and whose stomach lamentably empty, a few hours of morning and afternoon spent in the atmosphere of public disgrace, seem a whole age. I began to wonder, in a rather light-headed fashion, whether we had been in school about twelve hours, or if it were not really tomorrow, and if this awful day would ever come to an end. And then I became conscious of the well-known scuffling and shuffling which always accompanied break-up, and a few minutes later I was alone again with the tick of the clock and Mercator's Projection. I pressed my forehead against the desk in front of me, but found it difficult to think for the singing in my ears.

"Papa wants to speak to you in the

A Day of Punishment

parlour, Master Hyde," said a gentle voice from the doorway. I rose vaguely and followed the schoolmaster's daughter. I had only once been in the parlour before, and that was when my mother first brought me to school; I had then thought it a fascinating room, for it contained several large glass cases full of all manner of stuffed creatures, from a fox to a humming-bird, but I had no eye or heart for such things to-day.

Mr. Blocker was at tea with his wife; he put down his cup as I entered and looked at me over the tops of his spectacles. "I have been telling Mrs. Blocker," he said, "what a sad trouble you have been to your mother, and she is quite grieved to think of it."

I kept my eyes riveted on the engraving of the king in coronation robes which hung over the mantel, behind Mrs. Blocker, but I felt that she looked appealingly at her husband, and then at me, with a world of kindness in her eyes.

"I am glad to say, however," continued Mr. Blocker rather hurriedly, "that your punishment is now at an end, and I hope you will have benefited by it. I have been very sorry," he went on in a much kinder and a less professional tone, "very

A Day of Punishment

sorry, to have to make a public example of you to-day, but it was at the express desire of your friends, and I feel sure they would not have asked me to do so without due cause." I do not know if he expected me to reply, but I did not and could not, and after an awkward little pause he said, "There now, run along home, Harry, and make up for it all to-morrow."

I think I murmured "Thank you," at all events I got out of the room in some fashion.

"Poor little lad," I heard the motherly Mrs. Blocker saying, as I went down the passage, with my heart considerably softened towards the master, but no whit towards my home-folk.

On former occasions of real or imagined wrong, I had dreamed in the half-conscious romancing of self-pity, that I would run away for miles and miles; I would go to London and become that great and distinguished being I always vaguely meant to be, and then some day my people should hear of me again in my glory, and be sorry they had been so cross and thought so little of me, and then I would magnanimously forgive them and make them very rich, and take them to pantomimes twice a week. But to-night there was no play in

A Day of Punishment

my thoughts. I wandered vaguely out into the street, I had but one clear idea in my head, that I could not, would not, go home.

We had come through the greater part of October, and although the Pavilion clock had only just struck five, the darkness was settling down apace. The day had been curiously sultry for the time of year, but the evening for all its stillness was keen with autumn. As I stood there like a lost thing, a little inconsequent breeze came and boomed in my ears and lifted my hair pleasantly, and when it had passed I could hear the deep and gentle breathing of the sea : and that gave me a clue. I would drown myself, I thought, since there was no kindness or justice left for me in the world, since every one was turning against me, except my Father, whom I loved better than all the world, and who too would turn against me when they had raked up the old tales again.

There was certainly no play in my thought just then ; it was a very desperate little being indeed, that ran down the street and hurried over the beach till he stumbled over the stump of an old capstan, and fell and lay. How long I lay there pressing my cheek on the hard smooth

A Day of Punishment

stones, with no sound near save that of the tide I was waiting for, and the tempest of my own pulses, I do not know. But a sudden shock of deadly cold brought me to my feet in a second, washing away with it all thought of suicide. In a panic of cold, terror, and isolation I instinctively made for the blessed lights of the town, and, drenched to the very skin, blundered headlong up the beach, and found myself in a few minutes in sight of home.

I turned the handle of the door and slipped in softly, hoping to crawl up to bed without being observed. But Mary heard me, and called me by name, so I thought it best to walk with what dignity I could into the kitchen where she and Sukie were preparing supper for my Father.

"Why, what has kept you so long, child?" she said. I think in the fulness of her busy day she had forgotten the morning's storm. That is just the way with grown people. The event which fills a child's day with black tragedy is forgotten by them in the making of puddings, or the sewing on of buttons.

That was too much for me. In a last flare of blind passion I sent my satchel flying into one corner, flung my cap into another and tore at my shoestrings that

A Day of Punishment

my shoes might follow. At the very moment, however, the door leading from the office opened and closed : I heard the tramp of my Father's heavy boots, and his cheery voice calling my name. A moment later he entered the kitchen, peering about him rather blindly in the brightly lighted room, and after kissing Mary and inquiring of Sukie as to her earache, came over to where I stood with my shoes in my hand, like a fierce little beast at bay.

"Well, how's my boy?" he said, patting my head, and turning my face up with his hand. "How's my dear old lad, hey?"

O the loving hand and the kind, kind voice! There was no standing out possible for me any longer. I tumbled into his arms, and broke into crying with a kind of shriek. All the pent-up wrath, misery, starvation, and pain of that day came out in that passion of sobbing and tears.

"Why, boy, what's this?" said my Father startled, drawing me closer to him. "What does it all mean, Mary? There, lad, don't 'ee now, don't 'ee," he said, with a tremor in his voice, holding me ever closer and closer to him, and smoothing my hair with the big gentle hand.

A Day of Punishment

I have no notion what Mary or Mother, who had just entered, told him; my Father's kindness had opened the floodgates and I was carried out in spite of myself on the overwhelming tide, and could think of nothing, except that I was sorry, sorry, dreadfully sorry, and that I loved my Father, loved him so much that my heart was like to break. Neither do I know how it came about that a few minutes later I was sitting on his knee close to the fire, trying to please him by taking sips from his glass of hot wine and water, though the catching at my breath nearly choked me, and my tears rushed over the end of my nose into the glass: Mother was gently pulling from me my sea-drenched breeks, looking very anxiously at me the while, while Mary busied herself with warming me a basin of good soup.

I cried out in my dreams that night; and little wonder, for the terrible sea was coming up all round me, and I knew how cold it was; and my cry woke me. I lay and luxuriated a little in the sense of safety and comfort, and thought of my Father, and how he had held me so close and stroked my head as if he would never be done with comforting me: a memory that heaved up

A Day of Punishment

my little chest with a far happier sobbing, and I did not fall asleep again till I had made a compact with myself, never, so long as I lived, to do anything to grieve that dear and tender heart again.

MY PRETTY SISTER

THE first great sorrow in our house that I can remember was the death of my sister Esther.

I do not think I loved one sister better than another, but I was quite aware of their unlikeness. The story goes that, as I was one day sitting on Mr. Trevanion's knee, when he and the girls were chatting pleasantly together, I suddenly put my mouth to his ear and whispered, "I say, I

My Pretty Sister

think Mary is my *good* sister, and Esther is my *pretty* sister; don't you?" Of course he repeated my words aloud, and called forth a storm of make-believe indignation. I was a perfect little wretch, said Esther, rosily laughing and shaking her head; and if I would only use my eyes I might see that they had an equal share of comeliness, though she would not say as much for the goodness.

They might laugh at me, but there was some truth in my childish distinction, although both were indeed true-hearted girls and very good to look at. Esther brought sunshine and flowers into our homely life; Mary was its strength and its wit.

The love of the sisters for one another was very deep; I know this now, though I did not trouble my head about it then. Mary would have slaved from morning to night for Esther had the need arisen, and that without complaint, so great was her share of that elder sisterly love which holds at all costs to the faith that the young have a divine right to happiness. Esther's feeling for the sister only three years her senior, was touched with something near akin to reverence; more than ever so after Mr. Trevanion went away, and she strove so bravely to hide her sorrow.

My Pretty Sister

Esther was not strong enough to do much work about the house, so she used to help my Mother in her little glass and china shop in Ship Street, and my Mother used to say she was sure the customers

often bought more than they at first intended because of Esther's bright looks and pleasant manners. She was only seventeen, but she had a sweetheart, John Müller, a sailor, and a good fellow too. His mother's father was a German, who had played the fiddle in George IV.'s German band; and John had a touch of it in him, and could play with pretty feeling.

My Pretty Sister

Esther and he had been fast friends from her earliest childhood, and it was the most natural thing in the world that the old feeling should ripen into love, as soon as he left off going to school, and she got into long frocks.

Very shortly after Esther's seventeenth birthday John had to sail with his ship for a two years' absence. Esther was very downhearted during the few weeks preceding his departure, and her spirits told on her health. One morning I remember she said to Mary, with a little forced laugh, "I had such an odd dream last night," and then she went on to tell it. "I was in the shop serving a lady, and as she left another person entered, a strange veiled figure. I went forward and the figure put out its hand and said, 'I am coming to fetch you on the 15th of August,' and I shrank back and said, 'Oh, no, don't do that; that is my brother Harry's birthday'; and then it said, 'I shall come for you on the 15th of September,' and then I woke up.' Wasn't it a queer dream?"

"Yes, very queer," said Mary, rather abruptly, "and entirely due to your not eating enough, child, and being in low spirits. If I were you I should forget all about the silly thing, and eat a good breakfast."

My Pretty Sister

The night before John's ship sailed his mother gave a little dancing party, and Esther went, looking very pretty, in a light thin dress—a French muslin sprigged with rosebuds, Mary said; and she ought to know, for she spent near upon an hour brushing and doing her sister's hair, and tying her ribbons, and finally wrapping her up in thick shawls. After the dancing party, for which she had but little heart, poor maid, John brought her home, not by the shortest road, but along by the shore! There, no doubt, they could bid one another a hundred tearful farewells better than at our door.

Esther went to bed that night, and she never rose from it again; the chill night air had struck to her lungs through the thin dress, and she became very ill indeed, consumption rapidly developing from inflammation of the lungs. They moved her to the sunniest room in the house and she lay all day in her little white bed, turning her head towards the door whenever anyone entered, asking eagerly if any news of John had come yet? Alas! it was sad enough news when at last it came. Mother and Mary did all they could to account for the delay; a dozen times in the week Mary ran round to John's mother, always

My Pretty Sister

to find the poor widow still in suspense and longing for some word or sign. Weeks and weeks went by, and we had so often to say, " No, dear, not yet," that at last she gave up asking, merely looking at us with eyes of wistful inquiry. Mary was her willing and loving nurse and slave, always bright, patient, and gentle, and with no sign in face or manner of the grief that was wearing out her heart. My Mother, after her housework was over, would sit and tell her little bits of neighbours' gossip, scraps of news of the folks (often very distinguished personages), who came on the coach from London with my Father, and the girl lay and listened quietly enough, but ever when the door opened to admit another, her face flushed, and her eyes turned and craved for the news which was so long coming. As soon as ever my Father came off his coach, he would pull off his heavy boots and in stocking feet would come up the stairs to her room. "Well my pretty, well my sweetheart," he always began cheerily enough, and then sometimes broke down at the sight of her face, or the sound of the merciless cough, and left the room hastily ; sometimes he came to the bedside, and stroked his big, gentle hand over her bright hair, striving to speak

My Pretty Sister

but unable, only shaking his head. At such a time I have seen her make a pathetic effort to smile and draw the brown hand down, with her little white fingers, and press it to her lips. Other times, when perhaps the bright colour in her cheek led him to hope for returning health, he would sit in the rocking-chair by her bedside, showing her the flowers he had brought her from the great market in London, telling her of his horses—how the mare had cast a shoe just outside Horley and delayed the coach, how that old rascal Boxer was just as full of life and fun as if he were a chicken still. " Full of frisk and fun," he used to say, " and yet never a touch of vice, never all his life a touch of vice ; he'd be a perfect fine gentleman, if he wasn't more like an angel!" And then when the time came for her to take her food he begged Mary to let him give it to her ; he seemed so thankful to be able to do a little service for her, and would almost make her laugh, in his anxiety that she should take a whole jelly in place of her customary spoonful.

None of us ever spoke of John Müller now, indeed I had almost forgotten about him, and, childlike, certainly saw no connection between his absence and Esther's

My Pretty Sister

illness. Playing about in the street one day, I heard people saying he was drowned, the news had just come to his mother that the ship went down off Cape Finisterre, all hands lost. I felt very sorry at the moment, but I went on to school and forgot about it.

In the afternoon, a half-holiday, I went up to see Esther. The room was very sunny and hot, and the window was open; the ledge was but a foot from the ground, and it opened out on to the leads over the kitchen. This place Mother called " Harry's garden." We had no real garden; our little cobble-paved back yard, with its high walls, was only good for hanging out washing, but here on the leads were a great many flower pots, large and small, and a wooden box, and here flourished pansies, sweet william, musk, and a few straggling sweet peas. I was very fond of the flowers, and was their nominal guardian, and was very careful of them by fits and starts, but it was Mary (now that Esther could not do it) who again and again saved their poor little dependent lives, by watering them when they flagged for lack of care. To-day I determined to do my duty by them, and busied myself for some time in pulling off dead leaves and blooms, and collecting the snails that wrought such

My Pretty Sister

havoc among them. The question of insects, snails included, was a very puzzling one to me, for, naughty little lad as I was in many ways, I could never bear to hurt any creature. Too tender-hearted to kill the snails in question, I dropped them as gently as I could into a neighbour's garden.

I was happy and grubby enough to please any boy, and, occasionally putting my hot face inside the window to report to my sister what I was doing, was at last descried by Mary, who came in with her sewing in her hand to sit by her sister awhile. "Oh, you untidy little fellow!" she cried. "Here, come in with you; it will soon be tea-time, and I must scrub you down before you can come to table." And, indeed, it was true; for, what with the heat and the soil and the remains of the morning's school ink, I looked very, very disreputable indeed. I came in meekly, and she turned my little garments down to my waist and set to work with soap and water, Esther looking on with the shadow of a smile on her face; for, indeed, I must have looked a comical thing with my hot, red face and silver head and bare, skinny little arms and body. Mary rubbed, rinsed and polished, and talked the whole while, telling one piece of news after another in a way which I

My Pretty Sister

vaguely recognised as unusual; for Mary was no chatterbox, speaking but moderately, and always to the point.

Then of a sudden I remembered that I, too, had a piece of news to tell, and turning my head round towards the bed as well as I could with Mary screwing the corner of the towel into my ear, I said, "I say, Esther, do you know John Müller's drowned?"

No one spoke; Esther turned her head on the pillow away from us and lay quite still. Then Mary recovered herself, and before I knew, I was huddled out of the room, wet and soapy as I was, with a towel round my shoulders. "How could you? how could you?" said Mary, breathlessly, shaking me and glaring at me outside the door. "You wicked little fool, you!"

For a moment I believe she hated me. I was so miserable and frightened I rubbed the soap in my eyes and hid my face in the towel, and Mary returned softly and quickly to the room: the sisters were alone together for hours.

When I went to bed that night I wondered if Esther hated me and thought me wicked, and I was glad when Mary came and told me quite gently that Esther sent me a loving good night and a kiss and a

My Pretty Sister

little present to keep for her sake : it was a tiny, fat copy of the " Pilgrim's Progress," full of pictures, which she had greatly treasured as a child, and had often lent to me as a great treat on Sundays. Then Mary and I hugged each other without any words, and I fell happily asleep with the Pilgrim under my pillow.

My sister Esther hardly spoke at all after that, never wept, and never smiled, not even for my father. She just lay there for a few days longer, and then faded out of life. She died on September 15th. Mary said her heart was broken.

Chapter 7

OUR ODD-MEN

WE had some very queer fellows about us as porters and odd-men at one time or another. Sometimes they were poor shady characters whom my father thought to help to better ways, and not infrequently they were deaf or dumb, or a little gone in their wits; for, as my Father would say, a man must live even if he be knave or fool, and he would therefore always try to find some corner for them in his business. They were generally a rough, unsatisfactory crew; but in one point they differed in no wise from the best servants my Father ever had,

Our Odd-men

in their respect and liking of the Coachmaster.

One of the most respectable members of this quaint company was old German George, a great six-foot fellow, with a grand depth of chest, and a loud determined voice, with the ring of authority in it, come of the days when he was a sergeant in the Grenadiers. He had been carried off as a boy from his home in the Rhine Provinces to serve under Napoleon. A few years later, a French ship of war, on which he was undergoing his first pangs of sea-sickness, was captured by an English vessel, and he was pressed into the service of his Majesty King George. I asked him once how he liked being handed about from one nation to another, and he said, "If you will allow me to express the sentiments of my mind, sir" (this was a favourite expression with him), "I like to be an English soldier better than to be a French soldier; if I might be a German soldier and fight for my own country, that I would like the best." He saw a good deal of service, and was at the Battle of Corunna. Before he retired on his little pension and with his several medals, he had been raised to the rank of Sergeant-Major in the Grenadier Guards, and had

Our Odd-men

been regarded with some awe and not a little affection by the handful of men under him. He was a strict disciplinarian, and rigorous to the verge of harshness in the maintenance of sobriety, order, and a good appearance among his men. One of them, Tom Larkin, was a terrible pickle, and had strong leanings towards loose ways and pot-house pleasures. One day, Sergeant George having discovered Private Larkin's accoutrements and whole belongings in a state of neglect, felt that the time was ripe for action. Accordingly he traced Tom to his snug retreat in the "Jolly Shepherd," and found the fellow as merry as a cricket over his pot, and as impudent as you please. He merely grinned when he saw his sergeant enter, waved his mug in his face, and refused to budge from that place for Sergeant George or any other non-commissioned officer in his Majesty's service. Whereupon Sergeant George took the private in one hand, and a boot-jack (the only thing there handy for his purpose) in the other, he jammed his head between his knees, and, in his own words: " I did vop him, and vop him, and vop him, so dat he could not sit upon his chair during one week. And if I may be allowed to express the sentiments of my mind,"

Our Odd-men

went on the old fellow, " der vas not among my men no better man after dat time ; and der vas not a man dat did like me so much. O yes," he would sometimes add, " I did hurt him very much, and very hard ; but dat vas good for him, and much better than to be flogged ; some people would have flogged him, but that is a cruel thing for a man ; it disgraces him before the other men and before himself."

He was quite an old man when he came to us to eke out his little pay with such wage as an outside porter could earn. His great strength, and sobriety, and orderly ways soon raised him high in my Father's liking, and, indeed, brought him within the good favour of all who had to do with him. For us boys he was a living volume of tales of adventure and marvel, and feats of strength.

His loyalty to my Father carried him to great lengths at times. On one notable occasion the afternoon coach brought down two young dandified gentlemen from town, who by the guard's telling had made themselves sufficiently unpleasant to the other passengers the whole way down, and were now as full of importance as if they had been the King's brothers. " Coachman," cried one, with a great manner, " have my

Our Odd-men

luggage carried to 'The Old Ship': at once, mind you." George, laden with the baggage, went before to lead the way, but on hearing some lackadaisically insolent remark about "that old fool of a coachman," could bear with it no longer. He plumped the luggage down hard on either side of him and faced round on them. "Gentlemen," he said, with his stiff military salute, "if you will allow me to express the sentiments of my mind, it is oder people dat is a fool and not my good master. And, gentlemen, it will make me great pleasure to fight you bote." The story goes that the two fellows beat a hasty retreat in the end, and it was only George's strong sense of duty towards my Father that prevented him leaving the baggage in the middle of the footway.

Equally entertaining, but of a very different type, was Sprightly. He was not a regular porter receiving a regular wage, but a fellow who came in one day for an odd job, and engaged himself as a hanger-on, and would never leave us again. He was our Jack-of-all-trades, and whatever was the business in hand—a hamper to be packed, heavy furniture to be carried up steep stairs with a due regard for corners, or a message to be carried over the hills—

Our Odd-men

Sprightly was always the man to do it. Surly and insolent as he was only too often to the outer world, he ran to do the bidding of any of us, with the obedience of a slave and the devotion of a faithful dog.

He was odd to look upon, tall and thin, and with big bony limbs very loosely strung together. His red shaggy hair, and a something uncanny in his eyes, gave an impression of wildness, which was certainly not lessened by his costume. This consisted of whatsoever Fortune threw in his way; he had a quaint bit of pride in this matter, and I remember hearing him say more than once, " I may be a good-for-nothin' fellow and I know I ain't good for much, but I never did nor I never will wear a livery coat." One of the rare occasions that he appeared wearing a really suitable article of dress brought him into trouble with my Father, as a cross chance would have it, about that very thing. Some one had given him a white hat, such as was then very usually worn. With this upon his ruddy head he came into the office one morning, and it was evident he fancied himself hugely. It so happened that my Father, who had just been sadly put about by some stupidity of a stableman, came into the office at the very moment, in

Our Odd-men

that condition of pent grievance and irritation to which the least thing in the world may play the part of match to powder-barrel. Poor Sprightly's hat happening to be the first thing to catch his eye, the old gentleman exploded on that.

"What *do* you mean, sir," he roared, so suddenly that Sprightly visibly jumped, "by wearing that thing on your head? Take it off this very instant, and never let me see you in it again!"

I found Sprightly a little later meekly wrapping his beautiful hat in the *Brighton Herald*, preparatory to bartering it somewhere in the town for a different kind; and I could not help thinking the poor fellow had been crying about it, for all his six feet and the grey hair coming thickly among the carrots. My heart smote me and I went straight to my Father, who was now in high good humour and chatting with Mary over the tea-table.

"Father," I said, with all the gravity I could command, and with some little touch of reproach in my tone, "what is Sprightly to wear on his head?"

"Wear on his head? Why, his hat, I suppose," he said with the greatest innocence.

"You don't mind if he wears a white hat,

Our Odd-men

do you, Father? He has a very tidy one, and he is so proud of it."

"Bless the lad!" said my Father in his hearty way, "why should I mind? I'm sure he's welcome, poor fellow; he may wear what hat he pleases, white, blue, or red, if he will."

"But you seem to forget," chimed in Mary, "that you spoke so crossly to poor Sprightly about his new hat."

"No, did I then?" said the old man in a tone of great surprise. "Why, what an old bear I must be! And then to go and forget all about it, too," he added, shaking his head and with his eyes a-twinkle.

I told Sprightly what my Father had said, and before the "Alert" started next morning the coachmaster, with rather red face, be it said, found occasion to call him from his post at the horses' heads.

"Turn that rein over, boy — there, thank'ee," he said, adding hurriedly, "that's a very smart hat of yours, Sprightly, and suits you uncommon well."

Sprightly touched the hat in question several times and beamed with pleasure.

Several years before he came about our office he had been employed by two French milliners in Brighton. He had evidently served them well, for they complimented

Our Odd-men

him upon his speed in running their errands and told him he was very sprightly. He had evidently felt flattered by the little ladies' praise, for he adopted the sobriquet as if it were a title conferred by a queen, and wore it ever after. Few indeed were there among us who knew he had once answered to the more dignified name of James Humphreys.

If his name was odd, and his costume more so, his manners were a match for both. With any one of us he was almost invariably willing and obedient. I am sure he thought that we were the most remarkable family in England ; that my Father was by far the largest coach proprietor, his coaches the smartest on the road ; and as to his horses, Sprightly would have liked to know who could compete with them ! not the king himself, sir! I believe that even my brother and I, despite our teasing ways, which might have exasperated a less kindly soul, were very heroic young gentlemen in the simple fellow's eyes. Woe to that man who would have dared to say anything derogatory of us or our belongings in the hearing of Sprightly ! He would have stood as our champion against the world if need had been.

But he was a different creature to the

Our Odd-men

world outside our family : surly, dogged, impudent to those who did not understand him—a sullen sot, they called him ; and familiar to the height of impertinence with those who were very much his social superiors. I remember one instance of this, too amusing to miss telling.

A gentleman came into our office and asked permission to send Sprightly several miles across the downs to bear an important letter to his friend and fellow magistrate, Mr. Martin Hilyard, a gentleman of an old family, and a man greatly respected in our parts. After a little growling on the part of Sprightly, the gentleman sent him on his way somewhat soothed by the promise of three shillings to be awarded when he should return with the reply. The next day I asked Sprightly how he had fared. " Nicely, nicely," he said ; " they asked me into the hall and gave me some cold beef and ale, and presently out comes Martin Hilyard. ' Hullo! Mr. Sprightly,' says he. ' Hullo! Martin Hilyard,' says I, ' how be you ? ' And then he stood afore the fire chatting with me, and I says, ' I say, Martin Hilyard, do you remember the time when me and you went and got drunk together at the ' Pig and Pitcher ? ' and he laughed, and there was

Our Odd-men

two maids sewing in a room near, and they fell a-screaming with laughing when they heard me talking so with Martin Hilyard."

Boys are not so sensitive as girls; I do not think they so early become aware of the divine depths of love and pathos which surround their every-day path of life; they are not quite so quick to see beneath the comical exterior, the rugged speech, the small surface sins. Therefore what in Sprightly delighted us most, as boys, were his good nature, his readiness to enter into our sport, his comical doggy devotion, and the fun we got out of it. But I remember an incident which happened when I was still a lad, which opened my eyes to something in him better than all these things.

I had been very ill. They had once thought I could not possibly recover; but youth and a naturally good constitution were getting the best of it, and I was wearily beginning to drag myself up the hill of life, very languidly and with many a stop by the way. One afternoon I was lying in bed, in my little room, watching with half-closed eyes and drowsy head a fly on the window-pane, a forlorn straggler from summer, whose little form was surrounded by a small blur of mist on the pane. I suppose the creature was really

Our Odd-men

dead, but I remember thinking at the time that the fly probably felt just as I did; he evidently did not care to fly, or crawl, or walk across the ceiling upside down after the absurd manner of his kind, just as I did not care if I might never run, or jump, or whistle again; I only wanted to lie still and never move, or speak, or turn my eyes.

As I lay thus I heard some one coming upstairs, some one with very heavy boots, who was trying to walk softly in spite of them. The shuffling feet stayed outside my room, their owner gave a very gentle tap, and in answer to my languid "come in" the face of Sprightly appeared round the door. It was wreathed in smiles and kept nodding at me in a way I imagine calculated to cheer me up and encourage me.

"Hullo! Master Hal," he said, trying to soften his husky voice, just as he had tried to hush his heavy boots. Beg pardon, but I thought as I'd just look in an' see how you was getting on."

"I am better, thank you," I said, raising my heavy eyes to his.

"Aye, but you've had a bad time, Master Hal, a bad time, but you're getting on now, bain't you?"

Our Odd-men

"Yes I've been very ill, but I'm getting on now, thank you."

He disappeared and drew the door to, but a minute after, it reopened and Sprightly's voice, a trifle more husky than usual said, "I say Master Hal, don't I wish it would do you any good if somebody was to run twenty mile for you! Wouldn't old Spright be off!" Then the head was withdrawn and the door closed.

Sprightly had two besetting sins: he was a terrible fellow for drink, was poor Spright, and if we sent him to make a few purchases he never could bring home the correct amount of change! there was always a penny or threepence, or even sixpence missing, for which he, though with much head-scratching and general dolefulness of appearance, could never account. Not that he was dishonest, for he always made it up to us, either in coin at a later date, or in an unnecessarily large amount of work; but the immediate temptation of holding money in his hands was too strong to be resisted. Drink was the worst enemy of that half-developed, wholly devoted soul. How often have I seen him muddled and sottish, the foolish creature, at night, and groaning in sincere penitence in our office next morning! Especially well I

Our Odd-men

remember one night when he became so troublesome by reason of his drunken condition that I had to order him out of the place. "Get away, Spright," I said. "You're not fit to be with decent people, you good-for-nothing drunken fellow!"

"I'm a good-for-nothing drunken fellow, am I?" he said, in a stupid, unsteady voice. "Is that way—to shpeak to a genelman—Mr. Shprightly's poshishun?" He became very solemn and told me several times after that, that he could not stay. "All right," I said; "the sooner you go the better for us." But he would not be got rid of until I had shaken hands with him, after which he departed, remarking again in his maudlin manner, that he was never coming back.

The next morning, however, as my sister was sitting in the office totting up figures (she was my father's bookkeeper and clerk) she heard a great sigh; looking up she saw Sprightly standing before her with a rueful countenance.

"Well," she said tartly, remembering the annoyance of the previous evening, "I thought you said you were never coming back again?" Another groan from Sprightly. "You had better get along, and never show your face again after your

Our Odd-men

behaviour, your disgraceful behaviour, of last night."

There was a pause, then, " I say Miss Mary," he said, " you bain't angry with old Spright, be you ? "

" Oh, don't come talking to me, I'm too busy," she said, turning over the leaves of her book.

" I suppose you ain't got nothing for me to fetch or carry ? " he persisted very humbly.

" Well, there, go along," said my sister, " and carry that hamper to Mr. Smith at the other end of the town." And the poor fellow, quite radiant now, snatched it up and bolted for the door with the words, " You see if old Spright can't run ! "

People often said to me, " I cannot imagine what induces your father to keep that drunken rascal hanging about his office. " He is a disgrace to the place ! "

" Keep him," I laughed, " we don't keep him : but he won't go—he won't leave us, and besides he's not altogether a rascal." And so it was, he was never really engaged by my father as a porter, but he was always working for us one way or another, lifting weights that the others shrank from, running distances that would have killed most men, doing the marketing for my

Our Odd-men

mother—anything, everything, certainly as much for love as money.

Sprightly had a strong sense of humour which often got the better of what little courtesy he possessed. On one occasion our next-door neighbour, an enormously stout old gentleman, engaged Sprightly to do an errand for him, but complained that he was scarcely fit to go as a messenger in such a coat as he had on his back. This was a nondescript garment at all times, and was hardly improved by a recent spill of green paint over one sleeve.

"If you don't like my coat," said the terrible Sprightly, "you might give me one of your waistcoats. It 'd cut up into a whole suit for me."

The indignant old gentleman was choking with a desire to find a suitable reply to this insolence, but Sprightly gave him no time. "You're a nice one to talk, ain't ye? A great, big, bouncing, pot-belly like you!" And then, having worked himself into a real rage by now, he roared, "You're too big to be clothed, you ought to be thatched!" and flung out of the house.

His ever-varying impertinence to others and his absurd freaks about his own

Our Odd-men

person were endless, and we never knew in what fashion they would next appear.

One winter morning we awoke to find the snow had fallen fast and thick in the night. The coaching roads were in a terrible condition, and Sprightly was chosen on this occasion to go before the coach with a long pole sounding the roads, and gave rise to much mirth amongst the passengers by appearing suitably attired in an old huntsman's coat with a lady's lace collar round his neck. When the road became clearer and more passable Sprightly had a lift on the coach, and in this way travelled up to London. I heard the sequel from a friend of mine in the Metropolis. He was a very correct young man, a dandy in his quiet fashion. As he was walking down Fleet Street one afternoon he saw a crowd of people following an odd-looking figure, a tall thin man attired in a huntsman's coat and a lady's lace collar. Imagine the pleasure of my prim friend when he found himself accosted by this interesting scarecrow with, " Hullo, Mr. C——, is that you? How be you ? " and, looking up, recognised our man Sprightly.

Perhaps the strongest tie that kept Sprightly ever about us was my brother

Our Odd-men

Edward. He had never been strong as we younger ones were, and as he grew up he became gradually very delicate indeed. He was something of a student, and I think every one who knew him loved and revered that gentle spirit. Many and many a time he spoke to Sprightly when we others might only have laughed or appeared indifferent: the poor fellow took his words much to heart, and after Edward's lightest word of reproach, his remorse showed itself in an almost frantic anxiety to run errands for him.

But I do not think that any one of us realised how deep was this feeling until my brother died. Edward's death came upon us with sad suddenness, although for ever so long we had noticed the ever-increasing transparency and frailty of his look and bearing. He and his wife were living at Henfield, a little village about eleven miles from Brighton. They had been spending Christmas with us, and my mother was trying to persuade him to stay a few days more; he was restless and said no—he must get back, he must go home. Only *one* day more, pleaded my Mother, perhaps the weather would be warmer by then, and, besides, he was not feeling well, she was sure. Then the doctor who had

Our Odd-men

come in to see him urged him strongly to remain, "for I think it only right to tell you," said he, "that your health is very uncertain indeed; in fact, you probably have not very long to live." "Is that so?" asked Edward, surprised, but quite calm, "how strange! and yet I never felt better in my life;" and, then, as he still expressed the strongest desire to return, my brother Fred set off before him to make all things ready in the little cottage at Henfield. In due time Edward rose to go, kissed his father and mother, bade us all a kindly farewell, and stepping into the chaise, fell back dead. This is not the story of our family, else I could give a sad enough picture of the poor stricken parents, and the sudden gloom which obliterated all the Christmas joy of our little household.

Fred, after seeing that all was ready, and the fires burning well in the cottage, strolled out along the road in the direction from which he expected to meet the carriage. Great was his surprise at a sudden bend in the road to meet Sprightly coming full speed towards him. Breathless with running, the poor fellow could hardly gasp out the dreadful news he had run eleven miles to bring.

Fred was only a boy in his teens, and

Our Odd-men

the blow broke him down. He wept so piteously that Sprightly was scared out of his wits, and when he braced himself up and strove to run homewards he turned faint and sick. Then Sprightly, who knew how sorely my parents and sister needed him with them at such a time, took the poor lad upon his big, strong back, and so went, sometimes running, sometimes walking, until quite near home, when they met the cart that was sent to fetch them.

That was a terrible time; on every side we heard stories of the resurrection men and their ghastly work. But no thought of this horror stole across the sacredness of our sorrow. With tears and love, but with no fear, we laid my brother to rest in the churchyard. It was bitter cruel weather, and the churchyard lies on the side of a hill.

When the burial service was over, Sprightly came to Fred, and said: "I say, Master Fred, d'ye think the master 'ud lend me a box-coat for to-night?"

"What for, Spright?" he asked, thinking, perhaps, that one of the fellow's queer pranks would be strangely out of place just now.

"Well you see," he said, grinning in his

Our Odd-men

awkward fashion, "I thought, may be, I'd just watch by Master Edward up there on the hill to-night. I couldn't abear they should meddle with *him*."

We knew well enough what he meant, and procured a great coat and wraps for him; and for three long bitter winter nights the faithful fellow sat and watched by the dreary mound on the hill side. He had ever shown his affection in such ways.

"Sprightly," said my Mother, a little while after, "I may have said many a sharp word to you in my time—and I can't say I think the fault all on my own side—but I respect you for this, and I'll never forget it as long as I live. And Sprightly, I believe, yes I *do* believe he knows about it," and here the poor dear broke down and cried.

"Ah!" Sprightly said to me after one of his drunken bouts, "I'd have been a better fellow if Master Edward had lived."

The years went on, and each one found Sprightly further down the hill, for all my Father's kindly efforts to keep him decent and happy. Then I became very ill and had to go abroad, and when I came home I married and went to live in London. Then the railways came and ruined my dear old Father, and he had to leave the

Our Odd-men

office, and part with all the old servants who had lived about him so long.

In the thick of my hard-working life and its manifold new interests and anxieties, I lost touch with the old set for many a day, and I did not know what had become of Sprightly till I heard of his death. He had gone very much to the bad, they said.

I think he was at once the most grotesque and the most pathetic figure that ever crossed the little stage of my life, and I do not expect ever to meet with the like of him again. For he was a rare creature, and the queerest mingle of qualities: strong as a lion, tender as a woman, rude as a bear, forgiving as a dog, and as dissolute as any man in England,—poor old Sprightly!

Chapter 8

Sukie

WE boys always spoke of her as old Sukie, and indeed I thought she *was* very old, but have since realised that she cannot have been more than thirty when I first remember her. She was a fine wholesome peasant woman, with bright dark eyes, ruddy colouring, a hurried abrupt manner of speech, and a heart of sterling goodness. She came of an odd family. One of her brothers, a miller, had so great a disdain of such poor weaklings as suffered themselves to be buried in consecrated ground, that he determined to escape this fate at any cost: accordingly he erected a large marble sarcophagus in the middle of his field, and there after death they laid the remains of this whimsical fellow. Another brother was a maker of leather breeches;

Sukie

but neither of these, as far as we could learn, although they were very well to do, gave much towards the support of the old father, a little rheumatic cobbler, living in great cheerfulness, and poverty, in Pool Valley. Thither every Saturday night went Sukie, and it was the only walk she ever took. Although she had left her country home as a mere girl, and had lived with my mother ever since, she had never lost her first exaggerated terror of crossing roads, and going among streets full of strange people; or if she had lost it, she would not own to it, feeling it perhaps as a falling off from her cherished traditions and a concession to our corrupt and silly town notions. She took with her on these occasions half a crown from her week's wages, carefully wrapped in paper, and a dish of roast apples or some good thing from my mother's homely bounty; and in this way she supplemented his little earnings to the best of her power. I never heard her complain of the unfilial maker of leather breeches, and miller, for she had a proud brave heart; but their neglect of their father must have been an untold hurt and anger to her, for she loved the little old cobbler with a strong daughterly love, impassioned by pity. Sukie was with my

Sukie

parents for forty years and then she gave notice.

Ours was a very different household then to what it had been when I was a little lad. Esther was long since dead; Fred was working in France; William and his wife were both dead, and his two young boys had come to live with us. Mischievous lads they were, and kept the house in a racket from morn till bedtime; they literally brimmed over with an energy which seemed unable to expend itself out of doors, even with all the beach and the sea as a playground, and were ever on the grin over some plotting of practical jokes. Of all the household I think Sukie suffered most at their hands, and albeit I punished them as often as their tender-hearted elders would allow, there was no end to their daredevilries and carelessness below stairs, till even that faithful heart could bear it no longer. Sukie, with all her goodness, had a peppery temper, and then, too, she had from the first resented their coming into the house, feeling, very rightly, that the responsibility of such wild young lives was too great for the old people, and for Mary already overburdened with work and care.

My father was up in London; mother,

Sukie

Mary, and I were cosily talking round the fire before going to bed.

"Please, Mrs. Hyde," said Sukie, appearing suddenly at the parlour door, "I've come to say I want to leave."

We all three stared at her, stricken into silence by surprise. Sukie going to leave? Would the sea give notice, or was it possible that the sun would ever express a wish to resign his position? All the wholesome red and brown of her face was curiously blanched and her lips trembled. I noticed then, with a little pang, that Sukie was beginning to get old, so white was her hair about her temples, and the dark bright eyes more sunken than of old.

"Sukie!" murmured my mother at last, as if in a dream, and staring at her still.

"Yes, I know, ma'am," she began incoherently, and then she suddenly flared out with all the hot blood back in her face. "It's all along o' them boys; it's all the fault of them being here; and though the Almighty may hear me, I say it's all them boys!"

"But, Sukie," said Mary, pulling her wits together as quickly as she could, "we know, of course, how tiresome they are; but they are only boys, and you should not take what they say and do so much to

Sukie

heart; besides, you have had to deal with boys in the house before. I'm sure Master Fred and Harry here———"

"Master Harry and Fred!" cried Sukie, turning suddenly on me with a wonderful thrill and glow in the dear old face. "Why, when I think of them beside these brats, I could kiss the ground they trod on! If *these* are boys, they *weren't* boys, that's all I can say. Master Harry and Fred indeed! O Miss Mary!"

"It is very good of you to speak so, Sukie," I said, a little shamefacedly, for there rose before me in painful clearness a vision of Sukie, a few years before, going down the street on her weekly visit to her little old cobbler, with a large label bidding the public "Beware of the Dog" pinned to her unconscious back; and I bethought me of the terrible time when Fred and I leapt out upon her, from behind the door, so that she fell down, and, to our horror, cut her cheek.

"I fear it is only because it was so long ago that you think we were so much better," I added.

"No, no, Master Harry," said she softly, and shaking her head, "I remember well enough, I does, and it's just all the difference in the world."

Sukie

"I really think, Sukie," said Mary, with a little ring of offence in her voice, "you do not try to see the matter in a fair light. Here are these poor boys, orphans; they have no home but this. It is perfectly true, they are a little tax upon all of us, but I think we ought to try and help each other bear it; besides, they have very good hearts and will improve as they grow up."

Mary, like a great many admirable women who had been conscientiously strict as elder sisters, was blindly indulgent as an aunt, and continually surprised me by the excuses she coined for the boys, whereby they evaded chastisement.

"Of course it makes a good deal of difference when boys are orphans," I murmured, as in duty bound, after Mary; but with little result. Sukie only pulled her her lips in.

"Orphans they may be," she broke out again, "and I'm sorry for it. Maybe I'm too old to live with orphans; and I s'pose I am. As to improving, I should think anybody could see as I shall be driven into my grave long before they're improved out of their plaguy, teasing ways. No, I've tried it for Mrs. Hyde's sake, and for the sake of Mr. William as was, but it ain't no good; not a bit, I can't

Sukie

a-bear it, no, I can't," and there was a tremor of reminiscent anger in her voice.

"Well, Susan," said my mother uncertainly, laying down her knitting, and fumbling for her purse in one of her capacious pockets, "if you must you must; at least, I suppose so; do you want to go to-night?" She was thoroughly bewildered and her hands trembled curiously.

"No, no, Mrs. Hyde. I sha'n't go, I sha'n't leave till you've got another body to take my place!" said the old servant in a tone of would-be comfort.

"Take your place? O Susan, what will, what will your master say?" and here my mother began to cry.

"Aye, that's just it," said Sukie, hurriedly; I came to tell you now, because I couldn't a-bear to say it when Mr. Hyde was here: I couldn't a-bear to stand up to him and say it——" and she broke off suddenly and left the room.

When the matter came to the hearing of Sukie's brother, the maker of leather breeches, he very rightly invited her to come to be his housekeeper; and she, to our surprise, accepted his offer without question, and without enthusiasm. The truth is she was so dazed by this break with the little old world she had lived in

Sukie

so long, that she was reckless with indifference as to her future, and would have gone to keep house for old Harry, I believe, had he been first to invite her!

My Father was greatly affected when the time came for bidding Sukie good-bye, so, too, was my Mother; though she did a little scolding through her tears, and gave her to understand that *if* anything dreadful happened either to us or to her, there would be only Susan to blame for the desertion. And Mary said, " Remember, Sukie, if you are ever in any trouble, or if you feel unhappy, you will always find a home with us."

"Yes, Miss Mary, and thank you dearly; and I *do* hope as the new girl'll keep Mr. Hyde's boots nice, and don't you let your father and mother fret; you and me both knows their ways, and their wants, don't we?" and so on and on, in her excitement, chattered the good old soul, who had never before in all her life done so much talking.

And then for the last time she took Mary round the kitchen, showing her where every box and jar and platter might be found as she had left it in her exquisite orderly fashion. When she came to the many-shelved dresser, gay with our own

Sukie

willow-pattern service, her daily pride, she stopped and smoothed its check cloth lovingly. "I pray God the silly slut won't break much!" she said, and burst into tears.

We missed her sadly; the girl who came in to help Mary was a poor helpless thing, with a face incapable of expressing pleasure or thought, and her whole bearing utterly unresponsive to either kindliness or displeasure; the mark of the Benevolent Institution was upon her, body and soul. Very naturally she knew nothing of the long-established ways of our house, and felt no pride in it, or love of us. My father was much put about by the absence of Sukie; for forty years she had fallen in with the routine of his simple life, and the lack of her caused many a hitch in its working. One morning, I remember, I found him wandering helplessly about the kitchen with his neckcloth in his hand, when ordinarily he would have been mounting his seat on the coach. My Father's neckerchief being after the fashion of that day, about the size of a small dinner-cloth, needed so large a surface wheron it could be folded, that a special white deal-table had been set apart and consecrated to this use, and this alone, for as long a time as I could remember. But hither, all un-

Sukie

conscious of her error, had the little raw Martha brought her pan of water and her dish-clouts, and was busy rattling cups and saucers about.

"Do you know how late it is, Father?" I said as I entered the kitchen. He turned and looked at me; then he heaved a great sigh, and shook his head.

"Come here, boy," he said in a hoarse whisper, "Look at *that*, now!" he added sadly but indulgently, pointing with the hand from which the neckcloth trailed to the floor, at the shoulder-blades of the charity girl. "She don't understand, poor dear, poor dear, she don't understand." It had not occurred to him to enlighten her, and to claim his own; his nooks and corners in the household arrangements had from all time been ready for him, and he had always slipped into them without issuing orders or asking leave.

I quickly came to the rescue and told the girl of the mistake, and with a sigh of relief my Father set about folding his neckcloth in its customary place; but even then I heard him murmuring to himself in a soft surprised way as he went up the passage, "She doesn't know that! poor dear, poor dear!"

"O Sukie," I said, a few days later,

Sukie

when I called to see how she was getting on in her new world, and I spoke in a tone of sham despair, "you cannot imagine

what dreadful things happen now you have left us! Fancy, Sukie, my Father has nowhere to fold his cravat—Martha washes her greasy dishes on the white table now!"

Sukie

I was almost sorry I had carried the jest so far, for her face flushed painfully.

"O Master Harry," she said, and I saw I had given her a real stab. Then she shook her fist menacingly. "A nasty hussy!" she said, "O, I could, I could—I don't know what!"

"Don't be so fierce, Sukie," I laughed. "She is not so bad either. I was only in fun."

A few days later I called down the passage, "Martha, my Mother wants you."

"Coming, Master Harry," replied a familiar voice; and up comes Sukie in her white apron, and evidently prepared for business. There was a general cry of delight and surprise, and my Father jumped up and shook both her hands, and Mary gave her a hearty kiss.

"I thought as how I'd better come back after all," said Sukie, abruptly, her bonny old face all aglow with pleasure. Then my Mother, with an effort at severity, said,

"I am glad you have come to your senses, Susan," though in truth her whole person was radiant with the satisfaction she strove to conceal.

We did our best to keep the boys away from her and to lighten her burden in our house, and the faithful soul stayed with us

Sukie

till she was really too old for any more work. I was by this time a married man, and, when on a visit to our old home, asked her more than once when she was coming up to London to see my family.

"I'll come, sure enough, Master Harry," was her invariable answer, "for I'd dearly love to see you and Miss Lucy—(she always called my wife by her maiden name)—and the little ones. I'm only just waiting till they take them nasty screeching steam-engine trains off the road, and bring the coaches back; then I'll come sure enough, dear heart."

Sukie's working days were over. She went again to live with her brother, the leather-breeches maker, and there by his fireside she knitted and snapped and dozed away the last and only leisure days of her simple serviceable life.

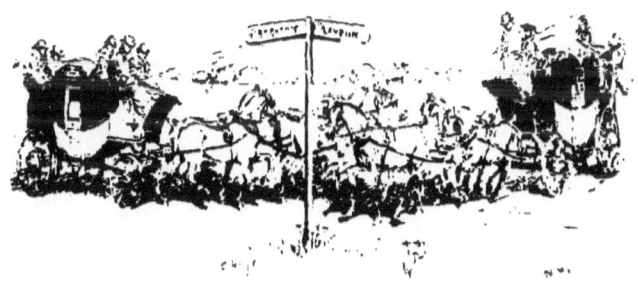

Printed by BALLANTYNE, HANSON & Co.
London & Edinburgh

*What matter though my novel theme appear
Rustic and homely to the town-bred ear?
Meet but for gossip of the village green,
Passion where'er she works is never mean.*

FORTHCOMING VOLUMES IN
The Arcady Library

LIFE IN ARCADIA
By J. S. FLETCHER
Illustrated by **PATTEN WILSON**

SCHOLAR GYPSIES
By JOHN BUCHAN
With Seven Full-page Etchings by
D. Y. CAMERON

1895.

List of Books
IN
BELLES LETTRES
(Including some Transfers)
Published by John Lane
𝕿𝖍𝖊 𝕭𝖔𝖉𝖑𝖊𝖞 𝕳𝖊𝖆𝖉
Vigo Street, London, W.

N.B.—The Authors and Publisher reserve the right of reprinting any book in this list if a new edition is called for, except in cases where a stipulation has been made to the contrary, and of printing a separate edition of any of the books for America irrespective of the numbers to which the English editions are limited. The numbers mentioned do not include copies sent to the public libraries, nor those sent for review.

Most of the books are published simultaneously in England and America, and in many instances the names of the American publishers are appended.

ADAMS (FRANCIS).
    ESSAYS IN MODERNITY. Cr. 8vo. 5s. net.   [*Shortly.*
    Chicago: Stone & Kimball.
    A CHILD OF THE AGE. (*See* KEYNOTES SERIES.)

ALLEN (GRANT).
    THE LOWER SLOPES: A Volume of Verse. With title-page and cover design by J. ILLINGWORTH KAY. 600 copies, cr. 8vo. 5s. net.
    Chicago: Stone & Kimball.
    THE WOMAN WHO DID. (*See* KEYNOTES SERIES.)
    THE BRITISH BARBARIANS. (*See* KEYNOTES SERIES.)

BAILEY (JOHN C.).
AN ANTHOLOGY OF ENGLISH ELEGIES. [*In preparation.*

BEARDSLEY (AUBREY).
THE STORY OF VENUS AND TANNHÄUSER, in which is set forth an exact account of the Manner of State held by Madam Venus, Goddess and Meretrix, under the famous Hörselberg, and containing the adventures of Tannhäuser in that place, his repentance, his journeying to Rome, and return to the loving mountain. By AUBREY BEARDSLEY. With 20 full-page illustrations, numerous ornaments, and a cover from the same hand. Sq. 16mo. 10s. 6d. net.
[*In preparation.*

BEDDOES (T. L.).
See GOSSE (EDMUND).

BEECHING (Rev. H. C.).
IN A GARDEN : Poems. With title-page and cover design by ROGER FRY. Cr. 8vo. 5s. net.
New York: Macmillan & Co.

BENSON (ARTHUR CHRISTOPHER).
LYRICS. Fcap. 8vo, buckram. 5s. net.
New York: Macmillan & Co.

BRIDGES (ROBERT).
SUPPRESSED CHAPTERS, AND OTHER BOOKISHNESS. Cr. 8vo, 3s. 6d. net.
New York : Charles Scribner's Sons.

BROTHERTON (MARY).
ROSEMARY FOR REMEMBRANCE. With title-page and cover design by WALTER WEST. Fcap. 8vo. 3s. 6d. net.

BUCHAN (JOHN).
MUSA PISCATRIX. [*In preparation.*

CAMPBELL (GERALD).
THE JONESES AND THE ASTERISKS. (*See* MAYFAIR SET.)

CASE (ROBERT).
AN ANTHOLOGY OF ENGLISH EPITHALAMIES.
[*In preparation.*

CASTLE (Mrs. EGERTON).
MY LITTLE LADY ANNE. (*See* PIERROT'S LIBRARY.)

CASTLE (EGERTON).
    See STEVENSON (ROBERT LOUIS).
CRAIG (R. MANIFOLD).
    THE SACRIFICE OF FOOLS: A Novel. Cr. 8vo. 4s. 6d. net.
                                                    [*In preparation.*
CRANE (WALTER).
    TOY BOOKS. Re-issue. Each with new cover-design and end papers. 9d. net.
    The three bound in one volume with a decorative cloth cover, end papers, and a newly-written and designed title-page and preface. 3s. 6d. net. i. This Little Pig. ii. The Fairy Ship. iii. King Luckieboy's Party.
    Chicago: Stone & Kimball.
CROSSE (VICTORIA).
    THE WOMAN WHO DIDN'T. (*See* KEYNOTES SERIES.)
DALMON (C. W.).
    SONG FAVOURS. With a title-page designed by J. P. DONNE. Sq. 16mo. 3s. 6d. net.
    Chicago: Way & Williams.
D'ARCY (ELLA).
    MONOCHROMES. (*See* KEYNOTES SERIES.)
DAVIDSON (JOHN).
    PLAYS: An Unhistorical Pastoral; A Romantic Farce; Bruce, a Chronicle Play; Smith, a Tragic Farce; Scaramouch in Naxos, a Pantomime. With a frontispiece and cover design by AUBREY BEARDSLEY. Printed at the Ballantyne Press. 500 copies, sm. 4to. 7s. 6d. net.
    Chicago: Stone & Kimball.
    FLEET STREET ECLOGUES. Fcap. 8vo, buckram 4s. 6d. net.
                                                    [*Third Edition.*
    FLEET STREET ECLOGUES. Second Series. Fcap. 8vo, buckram. 4s. 6d. net.
    A RANDOM ITINERARY AND A BALLAD. With a frontispiece and title-page by LAURENCE HOUSMAN. 600 copies. Fcap. 8vo, Irish Linen. 5s. net.
    Boston: Copeland & Day.
    BALLADS AND SONGS. With title-page designed by WALTER WEST. Fourth Edition. Fcap. 8vo, buckram. 5s. net
    Boston: Copeland & Day.
DAWE (W. CARLTON).
    YELLOW AND WHITE. (*See* KEYNOTES SERIES.)

DE TABLEY (LORD).
POEMS, DRAMATIC AND LYRICAL. By JOHN LEICESTER WARREN (Lord De Tabley). Illustrations and cover design by C. S. RICKETTS. 2nd edition, cr. 8vo. 7s. 6d. net.
New York: Macmillan & Co.
POEMS, DRAMATIC AND LYRICAL. 2nd series. uniform in binding with the former volume. Cr. 8vo. 5s. net.
New York: Macmillan & Co.

DIX (GERTRUDE).
THE GIRL FROM THE FARM. (See KEYNOTES SERIES.)

DOSTOIEVSKY (F.).
(See KEYNOTES SERIES, Vol. III.)

ECHEGARAY (JOSÉ).
See LYNCH (HANNAH).

EGERTON (GEORGE).
KEYNOTES. (See KEYNOTES SERIES.)
DISCORDS. (See KEYNOTES SERIES.)
YOUNG OFEG'S DITTIES. A translation from the Swedish of OLA HANSSON, with title-page and cover-design by AUBREY BEARDSLEY. Cr. 8vo. 3s. 6d. net.
Boston: Roberts Bros.

FARR (FLORENCE).
THE DANCING FAUN. (See KEYNOTES SERIES.)

FLEMING (GEORGE).
FOR PLAIN WOMEN ONLY. (See MAYFAIR SET.)

FLETCHER (J. S.).
THE WONDERFUL WAPENTAKE. By "A SON OF THE SOIL." With 18 full-page illustrations by J. A. SYMINGTON. Cr. 8vo. 5s. 6d. net.
Chicago: A. C. McClurg & Co.

FREDERIC (HAROLD).
MRS. ALBERT GRUNDY. (See MAYFAIR SET.)

GALE (NORMAN).
ORCHARD SONGS. With title-page and cover design by J. ILLINGWORTH KAY. Fcap. 8vo. Irish Linen. 5s. net.
Also a special edition limited in number on hand-made paper bound in English vellum. £1 1s. net.
New York: G. P. Putnam's Sons.

GARNETT (RICHARD).
POEMS. With title-page by J. ILLINGWORTH KAY. 350 copies, cr. 8vo. 5s. net.
Boston: Copeland & Day.
DANTE, PETRARCH, CAMOENS. CXXIV Sonnets rendered in English. Cr. 8vo. 5s. net. [In preparation.

GEARY (SIR NEVILL, BART.).
A LAWYER'S WIFE: A Novel. Cr. 8vo. 4s. 6d. net.
[In preparation.

GOSSE (EDMUND).
THE LETTERS OF THOMAS LOVELL BEDDOES. Now first edited. Pott 8vo. 5s. net.
Also 25 copies large paper. 12s. 6d. net.
New York: Macmillan & Co.

GRAHAME (KENNETH).
PAGAN PAPERS: A VOLUME OF ESSAYS. With title-page by AUBREY BEARDSLEY. Fcap. 8vo. 5s. net.
[Out of print at present.
Chicago: Stone & Kimball.
THE GOLDEN AGE. Cr. 8vo. 3s. 6d. net.
Chicago: Stone & Kimball.

GREENE (G. A.).
ITALIAN LYRISTS OF TO-DAY. Translations in the original metres from about 35 living Italian poets with bibliographical and biographical notes. Cr. 8vo. 5s. net.
New York: Macmillan & Co.

GREENWOOD (FREDERICK).
IMAGINATION IN DREAMS. Crown 8vo. 5s. net.
New York: Macmillan & Co.

HAKE (T. GORDON).
A SELECTION FROM HIS POEMS. Edited by Mrs. MEYNELL. With a portrait after D. G. ROSSETTI, and a cover design by GLEESON WHITE. Cr. 8vo. 5s. net.
Chicago: Stone & Kimball.

HANSSON (LAURA MARHOLM).
MODERN WOMEN: Six Psychological Sketches. [SOPHIA KOVALEVSKY, GEORGE EGERTON, ELEONORA DUSE, AMALIE SKRAM, MARIE BASHKIRTSEFF, A. EDGREN LEFFLER.] Translated from the German by HERMIONE RAMSDEN. Cr. 8vo. 3s. 6d. net. [In preparation.

HANSSON (OLA).
See EGERTON.

HARLAND (HENRY).
GREY ROSES. (*See* KEYNOTES SERIES.)

HAYES (ALFRED).
THE VALE OF ARDEN, AND OTHER POEMS. With a title-page and cover design by E. H. NEW. Fcap. 8vo. 3s. 6d. net.
Also 25 copies large paper. 15s. net.

HEINEMANN (WILLIAM).
THE FIRST STEP: A Dramatic Moment. Sm. 4to, 3s. 6d. net.

HOPPER (NORA).
BALLADS IN PROSE. With a title-page and cover by WALTER WEST. Sq. 16mo. 5s. net.
Boston: *Roberts Bros.*
A VOLUME OF POEMS. With title-page designed by PATTEN WILSON. Crown 8vo. 5s. net. [*In preparation.*

HOUSMAN (CLEMENCE).
THE WERE WOLF. With 6 full-page illustrations, title-page, and cover-design by LAURENCE HOUSMAN. Sq. 16mo. 3s. 6d. net.
Chicago: *Way & Williams.*

HOUSMAN (LAURENCE).
GREEN ARRAS: Poems. With illustrations by the Author. Cr. 8vo. 5s. net. [*In preparation.*

IRVING (LAURENCE).
GODEFROI AND YOLANDE: A Play. With 3 illustrations by AUBREY BEARDSLEY. Sm. 4to. 5s. net.
[*In preparation.*

JAMES (W. P.).
ROMANTIC PROFESSIONS: A volume of Essays. With title-page designed by J. ILLINGWORTH KAY. Cr. 8vo. 5s. net.
New York: *Macmillan & Co.*

JOHNSON (LIONEL).
THE ART OF THOMAS HARDY. Six Essays, with etched portrait by WM. STRANG, and Bibliography by JOHN LANE. Second edition, cr. 8vo. Buckram. 5s. 6d. net.
Also 150 copies, large paper, with proofs of the portrait. £1 1s. net.
New York: *Dodd, Mead & Co.*

JOHNSON (PAULINE).
THE WHITE WAMPUM: Poems. With title-page and cover designs by E. H. NEW. Cr. 8vo. 5s. net.
Boston: Lamson, Wolffe & Co.

JOHNSTONE (C. E.).
BALLADS OF BOY AND BEAK, with title-page designed by F. H. TOWNSEND. Sq. 32mo. 2s. net. [*In preparation.*

KEYNOTES SERIES.
Each volume with specially designed title-page by AUBREY BEARDSLEY. Cr. 8vo, cloth. 3s. 6d. net.

Vol. I. KEYNOTES. By GEORGE EGERTON.
[*Seventh edition now ready.*
Vol. II. THE DANCING FAUN. By FLORENCE FARR.
Vol. III. POOR FOLK. Translated from the Russian of F. DOSTOIEVSKY by LENA MILMAN, with a preface by GEORGE MOORE.
Vol. IV. A CHILD OF THE AGE. By FRANCIS ADAMS.
Vol. V. THE GREAT GOD PAN AND THE INMOST LIGHT. By ARTHUR MACHEN.
[*Second edition now ready.*
Vol. VI. DISCORDS. By GEORGE EGERTON.
[*Fourth edition now ready.*
Vol. VII. PRINCE ZALESKI. By M. P. SHIEL.
Vol. VIII. THE WOMAN WHO DID. By GRANT ALLEN.
[*Nineteenth edition now ready.*
Vol. IX. WOMEN'S TRAGEDIES. By H. D. LOWRY.
Vol. X. GREY ROSES. By HENRY HARLAND.
Vol. XI. AT THE FIRST CORNER, AND OTHER STORIES. By H. B. MARRIOTT WATSON.
Vol. XII. MONOCHROMES. By ELLA D'ARCY.
Vol. XIII. AT THE RELTON ARMS. By EVELYN SHARP.
Vol. XIV. THE GIRL FROM THE FARM. By GERTRUDE DIX. [*Second Edition now ready.*
Vol. XV. THE MIRROR OF MUSIC. By STANLEY V. MAKOWER.
Vol. XVI. YELLOW AND WHITE. By W. CARLTON DAWE.
Vol. XVII. THE MOUNTAIN LOVERS. By FIONA MACLEOD.
Vol. XVIII. THE WOMAN WHO DIDN'T. By VICTORIA CROSSE.
Vol. XIX. THE THREE IMPOSTORS. By ARTHUR MACHEN.
Vol. XX. NOBODY'S FAULT. By NETTA SYRETT.

KEYNOTES SERIES.
Vol. XXI. THE BRITISH BARBARIANS. By GRANT ALLEN.
The following are in preparation:
Vol. XXII. IN HOMESPUN. By E. NESBIT.
Vol. XXIII. PLATONIC AFFECTIONS. By JOHN SMITH.
Vol. XXIV. NETS FOR THE WIND. By UNA TAYLOR.
Vol. XXV. WHERE THE ATLANTIC MEETS THE LAND. By CALDWELL LIPSETT
Boston: Roberts Bros.

KING (*MAUDE EGERTON*)
ROUND ABOUT A BRIGHTON COACH OFFICE. With 30 Illustrations by LUCY KEMP-WELCH. Cr. 8vo. 5*s.* *net.*

LANDER (*HARRY*).
WEIGHED IN THE BALANCE: A Novel. Cr. 8vo. 4*s.* 6*d.* *net.*
[*In preparation.*

LANG (*ANDREW*).
See STODDART.

LEATHER (*R. K.*).
VERSES. 250 copies, fcap. 8vo. 3*s.* *net.*
Transferred by the Author to the present Publisher.

LE GALLIENNE (*RICHARD*).
PROSE FANCIES. With portrait of the Author by WILSON STEER. Fourth edition, cr. 8vo, purple cloth. 5*s.* *net.*
Also a limited large paper edition. 12*s.* 6*d.* *net.*
New York: G. P. Putnam's Sons.

THE BOOK BILLS OF NARCISSUS. An account rendered by RICHARD LE GALLIENNE. Third edition, with a new chapter and a frontispiece, cr. 8vo, purple cloth. 3*s.* 6*d.* *net.*
Also 50 copies on large paper. 8vo. 10*s.* 6*d.* *net.*
New York: G. P. Putnam's Sons.

ENGLISH POEMS. Fourth edition, revised, cr. 8vo, purple cloth. 4*s.* 6*d.* *net.*
Boston: Copeland & Day.

GEORGE MEREDITH: some Characteristics; with a Bibliography (much enlarged) by JOHN LANE, portrait, &c. Fourth edition, cr. 8vo, purple cloth. 5*s.* 6*d.* *net.*

THE RELIGION OF A LITERARY MAN. 5th thousand, cr. 8vo, purple cloth. 3*s.* 6*d.* *net.*
Also a special rubricated edition on hand-made paper, 8vo. 10*s.* 6*d.* *net.*
New York: G. P. Putnam's Sons.

LE GALLIENNE (RICHARD).
ROBERT LOUIS STEVENSON: An Elegy, and Other Poems, mainly personal. With etched title-page by D. Y. CAMERON. Cr. 8vo, purple cloth. 4s. 6d. net.
Also 75 copies on large paper. 8vo. 12s. 6d. net.
Boston: Copeland & Day.
RETROSPECTIVE REVIEWS: A Literary Log, 1891-1895. 2 vols., cr. 8vo, purple cloth. 9s. net. [*In preparation.*
New York: Dodd, Mead & Co.

LIPSETT (CALDWELL).
WHERE THE ATLANTIC MEETS THE LAND. (*See* KEYNOTES SERIES.)

LOWRY (H. D.).
WOMEN'S TRAGEDIES. (*See* KEYNOTES SERIES.)

LUCAS (WINIFRED).
A VOLUME OF POEMS. Fcap. 8vo. 4s. 6d. net.
[*In preparation.*

LYNCH (HANNAH).
THE GREAT GALEOTO AND FOLLY OR SAINTLINESS. Two Plays, from the Spanish of JOSÉ ECHEGARAY, with an Introduction. Sm. 4to. 5s. 6d. net.
Boston: Lamson, Wolffe & Co.

MACHEN (ARTHUR).
THE GREAT GOD PAN. (*See* KEYNOTES SERIES.)
THE THREE IMPOSTORS. (*See* KEYNOTES SERIES.)

MACLEOD (FIONA).
THE MOUNTAIN LOVERS. (*See* KEYNOTES SERIES.)

MAKOWER (STANLEY V.).
THE MIRROR OF MUSIC. (*See* KEYNOTES SERIES.)

MARZIALS (THEO.).
THE GALLERY OF PIGEONS, AND OTHER POEMS. Post 8vo. 4s. 6d. net. [*Very few remain.*
Transferred by the Author to the present Publisher.

MATHEW (FRANK).
THE WOOD OF THE BRAMBLES: A Novel. With title-page and cover design by PATTEN WILSON. Crown 8vo. 4s. 6d. net. [*In preparation.*

THE MAYFAIR SET.
Each volume fcap. 8vo. 3s. 6d. net.
Vol. I. THE AUTOBIOGRAPHY OF A BOY. Passages selected by his friend G. S. STREET. With a title-page designed by C. W. FURSE.
[*Fifth Edition now ready.*

THE MAYFAIR SET.
Vol. II. THE JONESES AND THE ASTERISKS: A Story in Monologue. By GERALD CAMPBELL. With a title-page and 6 illustrations by F. H. TOWNSEND.
[*Second Edition now ready.*
Vol. III. SELECT CONVERSATIONS WITH AN UNCLE, NOW EXTINCT. By H. G. WELLS. With a title-page by F. H. TOWNSEND.
The following are in preparation:
Vol. IV. FOR PLAIN WOMEN ONLY. By GEORGE FLEMING.
Vol. V. THE FEASTS OF AUTOLYCUS: The Diary of a Greedy Woman. Edited by ELIZABETH ROBINS PENNELL.
Vol. VI. MRS. ALBERT GRUNDY: Observations in Philistia. By HAROLD FREDERIC.
New York: The Merriam Co.

MEREDITH (GEORGE).
THE FIRST PUBLISHED PORTRAIT OF THIS AUTHOR, engraved on the wood by W. BISCOMBE GARDNER, after the painting by G. F. WATTS. Proof copies on Japanese vellum, signed by painter and engraver. £1 1s. *net.*

MEYNELL (MRS.), (ALICE C. THOMPSON).
POEMS. Fcap. 8vo. 3s. 6d. *net.* Third Edition. A few of the 50 large paper copies (1st edition) remain. 12s. 6d. *net.*
THE RHYTHM OF LIFE, AND OTHER ESSAYS. 2nd edition, fcap. 8vo. 3s. 6d. *net.* A few of the 50 large paper copies (1st edition) remain, 12s. 6d. *net.*
See also HAKE.

MILLER (JOAQUIN).
THE BUILDING OF THE CITY BEAUTIFUL. Fcap. 8vo With a decorated cover. 5s. *net.*
Chicago: Stone & Kimball.

MILMAN (LENA).
DOSTOIEVSKY'S POOR FOLK. (*See* KEYNOTES SERIES.)

MONKHOUSE (ALLAN).
BOOKS AND PLAYS: A VOLUME OF ESSAYS ON MEREDITH, BORROW, IBSEN AND OTHERS. 400 copies, crown 8vo. 5s. *net.*
Philadelphia: J. B. Lippincott Co.

MOORE (GEORGE).
(*See* KEYNOTES SERIES, Vol. III.)

NESBIT (E.).
A POMANDER OF VERSE. With a title-page and cover designed by LAURENCE HOUSMAN. Cr. 8vo. 5s. *net.*
Chicago: A. C. McClurg & Co.
IN HOMESPUN. (*See* KEYNOTES SERIES.)

NETTLESHIP (J. T.).
ROBERT BROWNING. Essays and Thoughts. Third edition, with a portrait, cr. 8vo. 5s. 6d. net.
New York: Chas. Scribner's Sons.

NOBLE (JAS. ASHCROFT).
THE SONNET IN ENGLAND, AND OTHER ESSAYS. Title-page and cover design by AUSTIN YOUNG. 600 copies, cr. 8vo. 5s. net. Also 50 copies, large paper, 12s. 6d. net.

O'SHAUGHNESSY (ARTHUR).
HIS LIFE AND HIS WORK. With selections from his Poems. By LOUISE CHANDLER MOULTON. Portrait and cover design, fcap. 8vo. 5s. net.
Chicago: Stone & Kimball.

OXFORD CHARACTERS.
A series of lithographed portraits by WILL ROTHENSTEIN, with text by F. YORK POWELL and others. To be issued monthly in term. Each number will contain two portraits. Parts I. to VII. ready. 200 sets only, folio, wrapper, 5s. net per part; 25 special large paper sets containing proof impressions of the portraits signed by the artist, 10s. 6d. net per part.

PENNELL (ELIZABETH ROBINS).
THE FEASTS OF AUTOLYCUS. (*See* MAYFAIR SET.)

PETERS (WM. THEODORE).
POSIES OUT OF RINGS. Sq. 16mo. 2s. net.
[*In preparation.*

PIERROT'S LIBRARY.
Each volume with title-page, cover-design, and end papers designed by AUBREY BEARDSLEY. Sq. 16mo. 2s. net.
The following are in preparation:
Vol. I. PIERROT. By H. DE VERE STACPOOLE.
Vol. II. MY LITTLE LADY ANNE. By MRS. EGERTON CASTLE.
Vol. III. DEATH, THE KNIGHT, AND THE LADY. By H. DE VERE STACPOOLE.
Vol. IV. SIMPLICITY. By A. T. G. PRICE.
Philadelphia: Henry Altemus.

PLARR (VICTOR).
IN THE DORIAN MOOD: Poems. Cr. 8vo. 5s. net.
[*In preparation.*

PRICE (A. T. G.).
SIMPLICITY. (*See* PIERROT'S LIBRARY.)

RADFORD (DOLLIE).
  SONGS, AND OTHER VERSES. With title-page designed by
    PATTEN WILSON. Fcap. 8vo. 4s. 6d. net.
  Philadelphia: J. B. Lippincott Co.
RAMSDEN (HERMIONE).
  See HANSSON.
RHYS (ERNEST).
  A LONDON ROSE, AND OTHER RHYMES. With title-page
    designed by SELWYN IMAGE. 350 copies, cr. 8vo.
    5s. net.
  New York: Dodd, Mead & Co.
RICKETTS (C. S.) AND C. H. SHANNON.
  HERO AND LEANDER. By CHRISTOPHER MARLOWE and
    GEORGE CHAPMAN. With borders, initials, and illustrations designed and engraved on the wood by C. S.
    RICKETTS and C. H. SHANNON. Bound in English
    vellum and gold. 200 copies only. 35s. net.
  Boston: Copeland & Day.
ROBERTSON (JOHN M.).
  ESSAYS TOWARDS A CRITICAL METHOD. (New Series.)
    Cr. 8vo. 5s. net. [In preparation.
ROBINSON (C. NEWTON).
  THE VIOL OF LOVE. With ornaments and cover design by
    LAURENCE HOUSMAN. Cr. 8vo. 5s. net.
  Boston: Lamson, Wolffe & Co.
ST. CYRES (LORD).
  THE LITTLE FLOWERS OF ST. FRANCIS. A new rendering
    into English of the FIORETTI DI SAN FRANCESCO. Cr.
    8vo. 5s. net. [In preparation.
SHARP (EVELYN).
  AT THE RELTON ARMS. (See KEYNOTES SERIES.)
SHIEL (M. P.).
  PRINCE ZALESKI. (See KEYNOTES SERIES.)
SMITH (JOHN).
  PLATONIC AFFECTIONS. (See KEYNOTES SERIES.)
STACPOOLE (H. DE VERE).
  PIERROT! A STORY. (See PIERROT'S LIBRARY.)
  DEATH, THE KNIGHT, AND THE LADY. (See PIERROT'S
    LIBRARY.)

STEVENSON (ROBERT LOUIS).
PRINCE OTTO : A Rendering in French by EGERTON CASTLE.
Cr. 8vo. 5s. *net.* [*In preparation.*
Also 100 copies on large paper, uniform in size with the Edinburgh Edition of the works.

A CHILD'S GARDEN OF VERSES. With nearly 100 illustrations by CHARLES ROBINSON. Cr. 8vo. 5s. *net.*
Also 150 copies on Japanese vellum. 21s. *net.*

STODDART (THOMAS TOD).
THE DEATH WAKE. With an introduction by ANDREW LANG. Fcap. 8vo. 5s. *net.*
Chicago: Way & Williams.

STREET (G. S.).
MINIATURES AND MOODS. Fcap. 8vo. 3s. *net.*
Transferred by the Author to the present Publisher.
THE AUTOBIOGRAPHY OF A BOY. (*See* MAYFAIR SET.)
New York: The Merriam Co.

QUALES EGO : a few remarks, in particular and at large. Fcap. 8vo, 3s. 6d. *net.* [*In preparation.*

SWETTENHAM (F. A.).
MALAY SKETCHES. With title and cover designs by PATTEN WILSON. Cr. 8vo. 5s. *net.*
New York: Macmillan & Co.

SYRETT (NETTA).
NOBODY'S FAULT. (*See* KEYNOTES SERIES.)

TABB (JOHN B.).
POEMS. Sq. 32mo. 4s. 6d. *net.*
Boston: Copeland & Day.

TAYLOR (UNA).
NETS FOR THE WIND. (*See* KEYNOTES SERIES.)

TENNYSON (FREDERICK).
POEMS OF THE DAY AND YEAR. With a title-page designed by PATTEN WILSON. Cr. 8vo. 5s. *net.*
Chicago: Stone & Kimball.

THIMM (C. A.).
A COMPLETE BIBLIOGRAPHY OF THE ART OF FENCE DUELLING, &c. With illustrations. [*In preparation.*

THOMPSON (FRANCIS).
POEMS. With frontispiece, title-page, and cover design by LAURENCE HOUSMAN. Fourth edition, pott 4to. 5s. *net.*
Boston: Copeland & Day.

THOMPSON (FRANCIS).
SISTER-SONGS: An Offering to Two Sisters. With frontispiece, title-page, and cover design by LAURENCE HOUSMAN. Pott 4to, buckram. 5s. net.
Boston: Copeland & Day.

THOREAU (HENRY DAVID).
POEMS OF NATURE. Selected and edited by HENRY S. SALT and FRANK B. SANBORN, with a title-page designed by PATTEN WILSON. Fcap. 8vo. 4s. 6d. net.
Boston and New York: Houghton, Mifflin & Co.

TYNAN HINKSON (KATHARINE).
CUCKOO SONGS. With title-page and cover design by LAURENCE HOUSMAN. Fcap. 8vo. 5s. net.
Boston: Copeland & Day.

MIRACLE PLAYS: OUR LORD'S COMING AND CHILDHOOD. With 6 illustrations title-page and cover design by PATTEN WILSON. Fcap. 8vo. 4s. 6d. net.
Chicago: Stone & Kimball.

WATSON (ROSAMUND MARRIOTT).
VESPERTILIA, AND OTHER POEMS. With title-page designed by R. ANNING BELL. Fcap. 8vo. 4s. 6d. net.
Chicago: Way & Williams.

A SUMMER NIGHT, AND OTHER POEMS. New Edition, with a decorative title-page. Fcap. 8vo. 3s. net.
Chicago: Way & Williams.

WATSON (H. B. MARRIOTT).
GALLOPING DICK. With title-page and cover design by PATTEN WILSON. Cr. 8vo, 4s. 6d. net.
Chicago: Stone & Kimball.

AT THE FIRST CORNER. (*See* KEYNOTES SERIES.)

WATSON (WILLIAM).
THE FATHER OF THE FOREST: AND OTHER POEMS. With new photogravure portrait of the author. Fcap. 8vo, 3s. 6d. net. 75 copies large paper, 10s. 6d. net.
Chicago: Stone & Kimball.

ODES, AND OTHER POEMS. Fourth Edition. Fcap. 8vo. 4s. 6d. net.
New York: Macmillan & Co.

THE ELOPING ANGELS: A CAPRICE. Second edition, sq. 16mo, buckram. 3s. 6d. net.
New York: Macmillan & Co.

WATSON (WILLIAM).
    EXCURSIONS IN CRITICISM; BEING SOME PROSE RECREATIONS OF A RHYMER. Second edition, cr. 8vo. 5*s. net.*
    New York: Macmillan & Co.
    THE PRINCE'S QUEST, AND OTHER POEMS. With a bibliographical note added. Second edition, fcap. 8vo. 4*s.* 6*d. net.*

WATT (FRANCIS).
    THE LAW'S LUMBER ROOM. Fcap. 8vo. 3*s.* 6*d. net.*
    Chicago: A. C. McClurg & Co.

WATTS (THEODORE).
    POEMS. Crown 8vo. 5*s. net.*   [*In preparation.*
    There will also be an Edition de Luxe *of this volume, printed at the Kelmscott Press.*

WELLS (H. G.).
    SELECT CONVERSATIONS WITH AN UNCLE. (*See* MAYFAIR SET.)

WHARTON (H. T.).
    SAPPHO. Memoir, text, selected renderings, and a literal translation by HENRY THORNTON WHARTON. With Three Illustrations in photogravure and a cover design by AUBREY BEARDSLEY. Fcap. 8vo. 7*s.* 6*d. net.*
    Chicago: A. C. McClurg & Co.

The Yellow Book

An Illustrated Quarterly. Pott 4to, 5s. net.

Volume I. April 1894, 272 pp., 15 Illustrations. [*Out of print.*

Volume II. July 1894, 364 pp., 23 Illustrations.

Volume III. October 1894, 280 pp., 15 Illustrations.

Volume IV. January 1895, 285 pp., 16 Illustrations.

Volume V. April 1895, 317 pp., 14 Illustrations.

Volume VI. July 1895, 335 pp., 16 Illustrations.

Volume VII. October 1895, 320 pp., 20 Illustrations.

    Boston; Copeland & Day.

www.ingramcontent.com/pod-product-compliance
Lightning Source LLC
Chambersburg PA
CBHW031746230426
43669CB00007B/510